THE GREAT EMBRACE

Trusting your life into God's arms,
so you can love yourself and others

TIM SISARICH

malcolm down
PUBLISHING

Copyright © 2017 Tim Sisarich

21 20 19 18 17 16   7 6 5 4 3 2 1

First published 2017 by Malcolm Down Publishing Ltd.
www.malcolmdown.co.uk

British Library Cataloguing in Publication Data
A catalogue record for this book is available from the British Library.

ISBN 978-1-910786-57-4

Cover design by Esther Kotecha
Cover illustration Jessica de Leeuwe

Printed in the UK

Endorsements

God is perfect, but the journey to know Him is very, very messy. In *The Great Embrace*, Tim takes us into his intimate journey to know the God he has trusted since childhood. His words will assure you that you're not alone in your pain, in your questions and in your hiding. Tim's journey will give you hope that God's mysterious love is worthy of a life-long pursuit. It's a beautiful work and I wish we had the luxury of sitting in a coffee shop, discussing what he's written.

Dr Juli Slattery
Clinical psychologist, co-founder of Authentic Intimacy

The Great Embrace is a powerful call for forgiveness and acceptance as pathways to a rich life anchored in faith and spiritual freedom. Tim Sisarich is both a humble and passionate writer, and his genuine love for all shines through his words.

Izzeldin Abuelaish
Author of *I Shall Not Hate: A Gaza Doctor's Journey on the Road to Peace and Human Dignity*

From the beginning of his work on Focus on the Family's documentary *Irreplaceable* to the completion of this excellent book, I have had the privilege of journeying with Tim along part of that road and sharing some of what I've learned and seen, too, as you'll read in these pages. Tim's humility is what grabs me most – his willingness to take the masks off and look at his own life squarely in the light of God's truth and God's mercy. If you struggle with hurt, pain and grief in your own life (who doesn't?), this book will be a source of great hope for you.

Christopher West
Author of *Fill These Hearts: God, Sex, and the Universal Longing*

Brokenness is part of the human condition for everyone—something Tim Sisarich well knows, as do I. Even those who depend on God will go through failures, experience shame, and feel guilt because of our sins and shortcomings. Thankfully, God's grace and power cover us and strengthen us to regroup and continue walking in faith. Tim is a fantastic guide through this process; his story illustrates these truths powerfully. Learn from his journey, and let him accompany you back to the feet of Christ.

Carey Casey
Ambassador for Fathers, National Center for Fathering

Contents

This book is written for the journeyman, the pilgrim, the searcher of God-spun gold. It is not the treasure, for that title belongs to Christ Himself. These are quite simply the ponderings of another, passing you by on the way. I have very intentionally drawn on the thinking and insight of others who have walked this path before us; theirs is wisdom that is far too precious to leave on a dusty old shelf. I have also drawn on my own experiences, but am still journeying too, looking for the same signposts you are. It is my sincere prayer that this brief moment together might cause you to pause and to ponder your own steps. May it be a hand on your shoulder, not to carry you, but to encourage you – for you are loved, and He is waiting, just for you… walk on…

Acknowledgements

There were so many people who pleaded with me to push on and finish writing, to push past the knock-backs from publishers and editors, the empty pages and the lonely days of writing. To all those pushers and pray-ers, especially Mary, Alistair and Rosie, thanks!

Thanks to every person who has ever brushed past me in life. Meeting and knowing you, talking and arguing with you, drawing from who you are has all been part of the shaping of who I am, how I think and how I see God and the world I live in. This book is for you.

I want to thank all those who have allowed me to quote them and to draw from them to create this book. I believe that we have so much to learn from all who have gone before us, and I hope and pray that as you read these pages, you might be inspired to search out those wiser than me, whose words fill a good portion of these pages.

Jesmae, my wife, has read every word on every page of this book dozens of times. Every rewrite, every tweak and every polish has gone past her desk. Without her patience, encouragement and unfiltered critiques, I don't think I ever would have started to write, let alone finish this book. In fact, I know that without you, Jesmae, I would have done very little of what I have done with my life.

Mum, Dad, Mark, Caroline, Chris and Anna, thanks for allowing me the freedom to share our story so frankly and honestly. I love you all incredibly and feel beyond blessed to have you as my family.

And finally Sarah Grace, Malcolm and the team at MD Publishing, thank you so, so very much! This book would still be deep inside my old Mac if it hadn't been for you. You have invested into me and into a story that I believe God dragged out of my heart and pushed up into my brain. Seriously, Sarah and Malcolm, I can't thank you enough!

Part One:
The Source of Pain

Chapter One:
An Introduction

All men dream, but not equally[1]
Lawrence of Arabia

On the morning of 2 October 2006, while I was busy preparing to host my daily radio show in New Zealand, the sounds of laughter and play filled the air around the simple, one-roomed schoolhouse in the tiny Amish community of Nickel Mines, in Lancaster County, Pennsylvania. Girls in their matching plain dresses and boys under their identical straw hats played happily and innocently, oblivious to any of the problems affecting the rest of the world. Little did anyone know then that the events that were to transpire that day inside that schoolhouse would become the tragic focus not just of my radio show, but hold the stunned attention of journalists from every single media outlet in the world.

Within an hour of that Polaroid© scene, Charles Carl Roberts had walked into the school and calmly instructed, 'Everyone to the front of the room. And get down!' He would allow the adults and the boys to leave the building before boarding up all the windows and doors and binding the remaining children – ten beautiful, innocent wee girls. And then, as police surrounded the building and Amish farmers knelt in prayer, Roberts walked to the front of the room and to that line of ten little girls, and as he approached, he raised one of the guns to his shoulder and pointed it.

'Shoot me first,' thirteen-year old Marian blurted out quickly.

'Shoot me next,' said her eleven-year-old sister, Barbie.

Gunshots rang out. Charles had listened. He shot Marian first.

... one, two, three shotgun blasts, then four, five six gunshots and they continued.

Police managed to smash their way in, but by the time they had, Charles Roberts had already taken his own life with a single shot. He was dead on the scene. Around him lay ten girls, all shot and bleeding.[2]

That October morning in 2006 left many, many people across the world asking again, 'How could a good God let something this tragic happen? These girls were His precious little ones!'

Why do bad things happen to good people? It's the age-old question, and the simple fact is that you don't have to look to some far-flung war zone or remember back to a distant holocaust or even shudder over the senseless and violent loss of those innocent, young lives in Lancaster County, Pennsylvania to see that we all live in a world overwhelmed with hurt. It knocks on the door of our own homes. Our past is riddled with its scars and shrapnel. And the trail of destruction can usually be tracked back to one or two people in our lives, who have damaged us in ways that trickle (or flood) into just about every aspect of our existence, tingeing every single choice we make.

I always felt that that *trail of destruction* wound its way back to the feet of my dad. I'll talk a bit more about this as we spend a little more time together. But essentially, he raised us in a home that outwardly had all the hallmarks of a strong, welcoming

Christian family. People would flock to hear him speak of the incredible works God had done in and through him; they would line up to hear God speak through him with words of incredible prophecy; God used him to identify and cast out demonic spirits, and I have never known a person who has led as many people to faith in Jesus Christ as he has. Yet behind the closed door of the home I grew up in, he was anything but welcoming. My mum did an amazing job shielding us from it, but the reality was that my father was a man filled with lies, anger, insecurity and had a constant battle with alcohol and womanising.

The man, who I saw others looking to for inspiration and hope, handed me a confused and distorted view of faith, life and spirituality. The man who had an almost 'superhero' ability with strangers seemed to hurt and crush those whom God had given him to love and protect. Bleakness and betrayal cast shadows over my future.

Yet, when you read the ancient writings of the Hebrew fathers of our faith, you discover something incredibly challenging, and yet equally beautiful... Moses, Abraham, David and countless, nameless others were faithful to God's call in their own lives. They too had anguish of soul, yet they said, ... *but God!*

Our infinitely merciful God wants more than anything else to see us whole and healthy and living a life filled with love... love for Him, a love for ourselves and a deep, genuine love for others. But before He helps us, our Creator is waiting for our permission to step in. The problem with this situation is that we first have to acknowledge a need for help... we have to come to a place where we are able to admit that our past is crippling our hearts and crushing our souls. Maybe unwittingly, we've allowed that hurt and pain to define us; to become infused into who we are, and how we see ourselves. Not only that, it also affects the way we let others see us and treat us. It even clouds our faith, clouds our view of God, and clouds how we perceive God should or would act for us and towards us.

The problem of looking back

But the problem of trying to live while still looking back at the past is really a double blow. Not only does it put us back into that place of yet again reliving the pain and anguish, but it also makes forgiveness nearly impossible. How can you forgive, when all you can feel are these old pangs? And that, right there, is the king hit – when we choose to live in the past, we become bound by the past, and bound to the very people we hold the resentment towards. These people become an idol in our lives and we give power to that idol… like a poison that runs through our very being!

Jesus, on the other hand, came up with a much better idea! Are you ready for it? He teaches us to cancel the debt! Yup… cancel the debt, and in return, Jesus tells us we'll be forgiven everything! What's more, He also tells us that if we can learn to forgive, our hearts will be set free. And isn't freedom from all the junk of our past the very thing we are so desperately seeking?

God teaches that your past was never meant to drown you. In fact, He declares that His plans for you are forward-focused… 'not for disaster, [but] to give you a future and a hope.'[3] These were never intended to be mere words of encouragement; the statement is an emphatic declaration, like an exclamation mark. What God was saying through His prophets! And that is the goal of this little book – to offer you H-O-P-E, which is essentially a feeling of trust and expectation that what is spoken will happen. I haven't come up with some secret formula; it's not a new message at all. Instead, I have made a point to spend my time searching out and then drawing from the deep well of the wisdom of our rich Christian heritage.

What I offer you through the pages of this book is the hand of a fellow pilgrim… a hand offered to help lift you to the hope on the other side of the fog of despair. It's my prayer that this new-found hope will give you a strength that will steady you, and encourage you to take a step forward in prayerful expectation into a life that is not removed from your past, but miraculously free of the shackles that came with it. And I pray that it will help you see that it is completely OK to question God. It's OK to expect Him to answer and it is also OK to expect that answer to unburden you. Are you not thirsting for that? Has not your heart and soul hungered for just a morsel?

My own spiritual bankruptcy and personal pain has caused me to stumble and crawl around in the darkness for too long. I am sick of living this way – and that has driven me, like you, to become a searcher of the truth too. I am desperate for God's light to inundate my life and enlighten my path. If you would join me on this journey, I am certain that together we'll start to see glimpses of Christ and discover that inner freedom the God-writers of old speak of, bringing us to that place of knowing that our scars and wounds are, in fact, marks of beauty, given by God. I will unpack this concept of our scars coming from the hand of God as we go through the book. And as I do, as I talk about issues and concepts that might fly in the face of your own theology or your own understanding of who God is or who God should be, can I encourage you to put the book down for a moment and have it out with God? That really is the heart behind writing this book… to create moments where we have to pause and ponder our hidden wounds. To take time to look back and contemplate the past that God Himself has always been a part of.

It's why, at the end of each chapter, I've added a final page that I've called 'Take Time', to give you some space. I really do encourage you to pause and ponder what we have talked about. I'll ask you a few questions and give you space to pray, to help you with some of my key thoughts on the chapter. Don't feel the need to rush onto the next page until you are ready. Let God gently draw you on because it's in these moments of wrestling and struggling that the power of God lives – where I earnestly pray the Creator of heaven and earth, the Lover of our souls gives you every ounce of encouragement that you need to put your hand in the hand of Christ Himself, and walk on.

The Bible tells us that God declares that He has a plan for each one of us, 'plans for your welfare, not for disaster, to give you a future and a hope.'[4] But those plans for our future also include picking up our cross and following Christ. That night before Jesus went to Calvary, He pleaded with His Father to find some other way, but declared, '… nevertheless, not My will, but Yours, be done.'[5] I love the way Eugene Peterson puts this in *The Message*: 'But please, not what I want. What do *you* want?'[6] It reflects the *pleading* desire of our Lord to let His Father do whatever He wanted to do, to bring the very best out of the situation He was facing. He saw what we also must learn to see – that God alone knows where each one of us needs to be planted, so that our past and our pain will bloom for His glory.

In their book *The Hidden Power of the Gospels: Four Questions, Four Paths, One Journey*, Alexander Shaia and Michelle Gaugy write that

Each of us has been marked by our lives. We can choose to identify the signs of these profound passages as 'wounds' – signs of our past (and sometimes present) suffering at the hands of others. We can use them to derive sympathy and attention and a sense of importance. Alternatively, we can choose to acknowledge them as the 'marks' that identify our singular humanity – significant and necessary parts of our journey. We can hide our 'marks,' or we can offer them up to others, when appropriate, so that those pathfinders can use them as trail signs while making their own way through the wilderness.[7]

All men dream: but not equally – those who dream by night in the dusty recesses of their minds wake in the day to find that it was vanity: but the dreamers of the day are dangerous men, for they may act their dream with open eyes, to make it possible.[8]

I pray that God Himself will not only inspire you to dream with your eyes open, but also enable you to act on that dream… a dream of living a new and better way – a way where forgiveness is real, where healing is total and where God alone charts the road you take.[9]

Take Time
~~~

- Take a moment to give this time to God. We are going to be challenged with some things that will hurt, and hurt a lot.
- In your own way, use this moment to ask God to prepare your heart and mind. Invite Him to speak into your life, as He desires. Allow Him to shine His light where He wills.
- Think about the person or people who have injured and hurt you, the walls you have built to protect yourself from them, and

lies and distortions that have robbed you of experiencing God's love. Use this time to plead for God's mercy and Spirit to carry you past the damage and over the walls. You probably won't feel it, but He is here to help your unbelief.

Pray

Our Father in heaven,
Reveal who you are.
Set the world right;
Do what's best—
as above, so below.
Keep us alive with three square meals.
Keep us forgiven with you and forgiving others.
Keep us safe from ourselves and the Devil.
You're in charge!
You can do anything you want!
You're ablaze in beauty!
Yes. Yes. Yes.[10]

Amen.

Chapter Two:
Know Where You've Come From

Know from where you come. Before you know who you are and
where you are going, you must know from where you come.[1]
Jewish proverb

My name is Tim Sisarich. My father's name is Warren Sisarich and
his father's name was Vladimir Sisarich. Vladimir left his mother
and his home of Podgora, an exquisite little Croatian village that
sits on the eastern edge of the Adriatic Sea, between the historic
walled town of Dubrovnik and the port city of Split. Long
before Croatia was an independent state, in a pre-Communist
Yugoslavia, my eighteen-year-old grandfather bravely boarded a
steamship bound for the bottom of the earth. The three-month
journey would cost him a year's wages and it would be more than
three decades before he could return to the place of his birth.
When he did finally make it back to Podgora, he was welcomed
with tears, heartache and the news that his mother died while he
was at sea on that return voyage.

My family traces the roots of the Sisarich name to 1801, when
a pregnant and unmarried girl, who was nicknamed Sisara, was
told that she could not pass on her family's name to her child.
The baby's father was a married man of high reputation, so there
was no way he was going to permit her to use his family's name
either. When this child was born, he was refused the identity

that was rightfully his. So he became Ante, the bastard son of Sisara, or Ante Sisarić. It was anglicised to Sisarich by the first generation of New Zealand Sisarichs.

With the name Sisarić comes the legacy on which it was founded. My grandfather lived with an unbendable pride and stubbornness that pushed him to work so many hours that his kids never saw him. He was determined that he would be someone, that his own children would go to the best schools and universities and find the best jobs... they were Sisarichs, and as far as he could help it, never again would anyone look down on the son of a Sisarich! That fight to be worthy, to be accepted, had been passed on from generation to generation.

And it didn't stop there

That pride was the cause of my father's biggest disaster and my greatest pain. Warren Sisarich, another proud son of Sisara, went on to repeat the cycle. The fact that he had the best education his parents could afford, that he went to a great university and became a partner in a fantastic legal firm just weren't enough for him. He was so determined to show the world that Warren Sisarich was someone, that my dad basically gambled away his life, eventually stealing money from his clients to cover huge gambling debts. That led to a prison sentence and a life of shame and pain that compounded his drive to prove himself. The stress drove him to drink, and drink a lot! Then, as a drunk, shame-filled shell of a Sisarich, he would try to fill his life with sexual conquests. Those countless drunken nights left a trail of devastation in the home of my youth.

I didn't know it then, but when I was eight years old, the woman with whom he was having an affair become pregnant with his child. It's with a huge amount of sadness that I write these words. She was repeating my family's story, pregnant with another unwanted, unnamed son of Sisara. While we knew my dad had *shared the love*, so to speak, it would be almost three decades before we'd even know that we had half-brother.

Twenty-nine years after that child was born, as I am writing these words, I am actually going to get the opportunity to meet that unknown brother, that unwanted son, for the very first time. The experience of writing these thoughts down is forcing me to confront a past that, for the longest time, I haven't wanted to touch. The pain it caused me, the pain that it continues to cause my mum, and the damage done to my newly discovered half-brother, my own flesh and blood, has been too much. I have carried the guilt that I could have, and should have, done something sooner to help him become part of the family in which he belongs, as a wanted son of Sisara.

I know that sharing this aspect of my family's story is the perfect launch pad to create some profound sermon point of how God has worked it all out for some amazing *happily-ever-after* good. But I'm not at that place yet – I'm still working through my own stuff.

When I was thirteen years old, I made a $10 bet with a friend that one day my face would be on the cover of a magazine. I went through my teens and twenties desperate to be someone, to have significance, to count. Amongst the rest of the chaos in their lives, caused largely by my dad's alcoholism, compulsive gambling, womanising and explosive temper, my parents had been married for a little less than a year when my oldest brother was born. By the time I was ready to leave high school, they'd had almost thirty years of children dominating their lives and their home.

Because my dad was so busy trying to prove himself to a world that he could never really please, I was always left with the feeling that he never loved me or that he could never show me any sort of genuine love. There was a whole lot of trouble and strife filling those three decades, so I grew up thinking that I was cramping my parents' relationship. As a confused and insecure teenager, I never saw my dad's issues as the cause of their marital ups and downs. I thought that I was the problem. I mean, there's no way a couple can find time to sort out an embittered marriage when you've always had kids cramping the healing, right?

From what I could see, there was no chance for them to get to know each other, to get past the damage that had already plagued them. Like my father, his father and almost every generation of Sisarich back to Ante, my life is marked with a deeply ingrained sense that I didn't really belong. This created in me a distorted need to be noticed, to be seen as someone of value. I was so desperate to be part of a community that cared for me in a way that I had constructed in my mind as perfect. I would look for it in girlfriends, in the 'right' groups of friends; I would throw myself into any group I could in the hope it was *the one.* I have spent my whole adult life trying desperately, yet without success, to find that illusion of identity in Church-based endeavours. I tried connecting to strong Christian leaders, I tried missions and ministry... I became a servant to anyone who appeared to capture what I thought represented the idea of a strong, godly leader. And every single one of those experiences led to even more disappointment for me. I spent years pushing, pulling and dragging my wife and five young children around behind me, as I earnestly tried to create an identity that my own father failed to build into me. But I have failed too. I have spent so much of my life trying to prove my worth and then bashing myself around because of the realisation that I'm just as guilty of repeating the

Sisarich cycle. I have always wanted to run from that life, to die to that person and become someone new – the new life that's supposed to come to the Christian soul, free of the pain of my childhood and of the pain handed down to me in the form of the legacy of Warren Sisarich.

But here is how God sees the story

God declares that all of this mess is actually part my identity; it is part of who I am. It doesn't matter whether I like the fact that my forefather was an unwanted bastard child. I would imagine that that poor solo mum of his probably never dreamt, back in 1801, that her anguish would become her ongoing legacy. I'd also bet that the boy, born with no name, would never have thought that he would live on as father of at least seven generations of Sisarić sons and daughters, or that his story would be part of a book written to help others find their name. And that name, my friend, *is loved and favoured child of God!*

I'm not for a second suggesting that my story is in any way unique to this kid from a blink-and-you-miss-it town on the bottom side of the world. Unhappiness and pain litter society. Our history is built on the back of personal agony. What's an even worse heartbreak is that *the Church* is just as tortured by the individual pasts that seem to plague us, no matter how often we lay them down at the foot of the cross.

That's the very reason why so much of our lives is absorbed by social media and why, before social media, we devoured all those trashy weeklies. They give us a peek into the lives of the rich and the famous. I know that we're not supposed to say this sort of stuff out loud, but we all desperately want at least a glimmer of the illusion, which the filters that Photoshop© uses have created, in our own lives. Yet why is it that the perceived happiness that flickers on a screen is always so elusive? Why is it that we real people are left limping through our lives, each loaded up with the junk of a life that no one else ever seems to really understand?

Why is it that, as one woman I interviewed for this book put it, 'we go round and round in circles, coming back to that same place of having to "forgive and let go, or the feelings destroy you" … but it will never fully go away'?

It does appear, for so many of us, that no matter how much prayer or church or praise and worship we fill our lives with, still we are somehow left with a damaged present because of a wounded past. It would seem that there's just no escape from the hate or the anger, or the guilt or the pain that is, more often than not, caused by someone else's sin or stupidity.

The result, if you are anything like me, leaves you screaming out into the heavens or whispering through tears: 'Why, God? Why? WHY?' It doesn't matter where I go or who I talk to, everyone seems to have their own experiences that bring each of us back to that agonising *Why?* Through my time in media, I have come across story after story and person after person who looked me in the eyes and pleaded for the answer.

The answer to questions like:

'Why did I have to be the one to cop the disgustingly cruel torment that my grandfather forced upon me when I was a child? And why are the effects of it still robbing me of the happiness I deserve? Where was God then and where is He now?'

'Why did I have to have my life wrecked because of the sexual abuse of my brother? It wasn't even my fault! I couldn't do anything to stop it!'

'Why did the selfishness of my father have to ruin my chances at personal happiness? If he had fought for me when I was most vulnerable, I wouldn't be sitting in the misery of the poor life choices I made because of it!'

'Why can't my husband have eyes only for me? Why can't he stay out of the beds of other women? And why am I too ashamed to leave him? Surely, I deserve better?'

'Why did God have to take my husband, my son and my father? A woman should never have to bury the three most important men in her life in the same year!'

'Why did my mum have to walk out on my dad and leave me as the only one to hold the family together?'

Each one of those statements comes from a real person, desperately seeking answers to questions that have impacted their own lives... questions that reveal the shadows of very real pain. I recall each face, each person. And as I sat and looked into their eyes, I wished that I'd had some kind of hope-filled, life-giving answer. In the more than twenty years I have been involved in media, I have spoken to and interviewed countless people whose lives have become completely consumed by the pain or hurt or damage caused to them.

By the way, I wouldn't have asked all those questions or undertaken any of the interviews had I not been seeking the answer to that now squeaky door of a question: Why does all the rubbish of life seem to land in the lives of good people? I have battled during my lifetime with the actions and choices of my own dad, and with how to handle the effects of those on my own life and life choices.

My prayer of hope

I wish so much that someone had told me back then what I've come to see – the beautiful miracle of the hopeful. And it's my prayer that as you turn the pages of this book, God leads you by His faultless grace to a place where you can see yourself as you really are… as He sees you; that you learn to see the divine beauty in your situation. I want to know, from personal experience, what it means to experience that grace, reflected through a genuinely hope-filled life.

At this point in your life it may seem impossible to see that there really is a light in your darkness. But the Bible shows us that God truly is a good God; He is a God who loves each one of us to bits.

He wants us to experience this for ourselves, not just read about it in the pages of another's autobiography. So as we set out together, as we spend this time together, I pray that God would take this dimly lit fact and cause it to become more and more clear, more and more deeply rooted in our lives. I pray that our heavenly Father would bring us to the point of not just being able to say the words, but to truly, truly believe that He is already at work in our lives, using all the bad that we have been forced to endure, for our good and for our blessing.

I'm not going to lie, it ain't gonna be an easy journey. But I truly believe that the mountaintop God our Father is leading us to has views that will be absolutely life-changingly beautiful. If you have the courage to walk it, you too will echo the now-famous words of one of the twentieth century's greatest men, Nelson Mandela, who in his autobiography, *Long Walk to Freedom*, said this:

I have walked that long road to freedom. I have tried not to falter; I have made missteps along the way. But I have discovered the secret that after climbing a great hill, one only finds that there are many more hills to climb. I have taken a moment here to rest, to steal a view of the glorious vista that surrounds me, to look back on the distance I have come.[2]

Over his lifetime, Mandela lived many lives – that of a lawyer, an anti-apartheid revolutionary (remember, one man's revolutionary is another's terrorist), then he went on to become a politician and statesman as well as a husband, father and friend. In the 1960s, fighting shameful injustices, Mandela was arrested and sentenced to life imprisonment for conspiracy to overthrow the state. For the next twenty-seven years his home was a damp, eight by seven foot concrete cell with a straw mat as a bed. He spent his days working in a lime quarry, where (oddly) it was forbidden for him to wear sunglasses, permanently damaging his eyesight. The system permitted him one visitor and one letter every six months. After his release, Nelson Mandela became the man who united a sorely divided nation, becoming South Africa's first black President and creating the Truth and Reconciliation Commission,[3] which saw forgiveness and repentance happen on a scale that I'd suggest the world has never before seen or experienced. He was awarded the Nobel Peace Prize in 1993.

One of the most important things we can learn from the man who is often referred to as *Tata* or 'Father' by the people of South Africa is that he understood the importance to 'look back on the distance I have come'. He realised that, like all of us, before you know who you are and where you are going, you must know from whence you came. As surprising as it might seem, the answers to our hope-filled future are hidden in the buried pain of our past. So if that is, in fact, true, then unless we turn back and learn how *not* to hate the hurter, we will be forever cursed with the forced labour of the impossible climb up a never-ending mountain, in the vain hope of glimpsing an illusion of happiness. Mandela saw this too, closing his biography by saying, 'I dare not linger; for my long walk is not yet ended.'[4]

Take Time

- Writing this has caused me to confront the pain of my childhood and take an honest look at how it has shaped and impacted my life's choices. Take some time to do the same with your own story. Make some notes if it helps. Allow God's Spirit to breathe healing on you and your story.
- Pain has a tendency to blind us to reality. Allow yourself to take an honest assessment of how your brokenness has distorted the truths of God in your life – you are loved; you are precious; you have a purpose. Can you see any glimpses of God's hand in the good *and* bad of your story? Write down what you hear. Be honest too. But don't move on until God gives you even a flicker of His hope for who you are.
- Ask God to prepare your heart for what He has in store for you during the next few chapters.

Pray

God, please lead me by your faultless grace to a place where I can see myself as I really am… as You see me. I pray that as I look back at my pain and scars, You would help me see Your divine beauty and purpose in my situation. I want to know, from personal experience, what it means to experience a genuinely hope-filled life.

Amen.

Chapter Three:
Unattainable Desires

The good God would not inspire unattainable desires.[1]
St Therese of Lisieux

I know it's ultimately what we want, but unfortunately, there's no easy 'Just read this book, repeat three times and you'll be fine' kind of solution to this journey of ours. That's what makes Mandela's *Long Walk to Freedom* so poignant. But I don't say that to discourage going forward, because what you and I have to hold on to, without any reservation at all, is that if the Bible says 'we know that in all things God works for the good of those who love him',[2] then not only is this true, but also God expects us to take him at His word.

The door opens to genuine healing

It really doesn't matter how you choose to slice that verse or which version you read; at the end of the day, it says exactly the same thing – God causes everything to work for our good. He is *not* saying that despite all the garbage He *can* use our lives for the good of others, although that is in there as a byproduct. When it comes to your life, your hurt and the giver of that hurt, I hear God saying:

I am your guide on this journey. I made the path you are

walking on. I see a much bigger picture… the secret is that you have to trust that I know what is best for you. I will lead you in that best way, if you would trust Me and let Me lead you. I will use your life and I will use your past and your pain for your good… just as I have always done.

The flip side is also true – God is trying to awaken each of us to the hard-to-chew reality that if we don't allow Him to *turn our hearts* and to bring us to a place of healing where the pain-makers in our lives are concerned, the Bible says that we're actually bringing a curse on ourselves.[3] Can you get a hold of that point? This isn't about minimising your scars or wounds, but rather it allows us to see that before us stands a door. And that door opens in a place of genuine healing.

Essentially, we can choose to let the suffering that has shaped so much of who we are, be a curse and a noose to us – or we can choose the door God has set before us and let God use everything in our life just as He intends. If we can do that right now, in this instant, even if we don't fully believe it yet, we'll discover that it will become a way for us to embrace who we are. I am certain that if we can do that, no matter how hard it might be, we will discover how to let God take our past and our pain, and we will see Him give it all back to us as an incredibly powerful tool for our good. The choice for change, however, sits with each of us to make.

Sit with this one thought; let it linger in your consciousness; sit with it until you catch it. It is such an important revelation that will change your entire life and reason for living… That God is over all things, in all things, through all things and behind all things. And because He knows each of us individually, He knows the very best way for each of us to make our way to heaven's gates.

That revelation is pretty new for me, happening during the 15 months I spent making *Irreplaceable*,[4] a documentary on God's design and purpose of family. I was travelling across the globe, talking with different experts about why family and everything associated with it was disintegrating. Without really realising it, I was trying to build a case against my dad; trying to stack up the evidence that pointed back to *Fatherlessness* being the primary reason society in the twenty-first century seems to be crumbling. I wanted a reason to pin my father to the wall, so to speak, and throw the cold hard facts at him.

It really is a choice

I felt sure that if I could prove that it was his fault my self-worth wasn't what it should be, that it was his fault I didn't finish university, that it was his fault I struggled with pornography, struggled as a husband and father myself, then I'd be somehow free. But I have come to realise that I was chasing the wind of lies! It's true that the damage caused to you, even by a single person, may well have defined you. It has shaped and labelled so many of us: crippled us, too. But if we could be really, truly honest, we'd see that that's because we have *chosen* to wrap ourselves in the pain, like a cloak.

Unless we can embrace our lives, with all the cracks and chips and busted-up-ness, it will continue to blur us from the reality of who we are – that we, you and me, are loved by God, wrapped up in His cloak of loving-kindness and of healing.

This idea of fully and totally letting God in, and allowing Him complete access to all the hidden places of my past really scared me. I was terrified that He might open all of my insecurities, fears and lies for all the world to see… that everyone would finally know the truth – Tim Sisarich is worthless, unwanted and unacceptable. I was so scared that once that happened, even Jesmae (my wife) wouldn't want me anymore, she'd kick me to the kerb, where I belonged.

My secret fear was that God would show the world I was, in fact, some loser who had constructed a grand house of cards to hide in. But what I am discovering, as I take the time to look and listen to what He is actually saying and what He wants me to actually hear, through the words of the prophets, apostles and holy men and women throughout the centuries, is that He never wanted me grovelling around at His feet finding joy in the crumbs from under His table.

No! God is not waiting for me to achieve just a little bit more, or maybe to go back to who I was before life wrecked me. It's the opposite, actually. He loves me so much and He chose me to be exactly who I am today. He knew, before the foundation of the world, who I would grow to be. He knew *all* of the life that I was going to live. He knew all about that pain too. He foresaw all of that. He also knew how all those experiences were going to shape me. And here's the kicker: He still loves me! God loves me (to summarise Brennan Manning) for who I am, not who I could be; He loves me for who I am, not who I should be.

Don't let that statement breeze by as just a nice little bumper sticker slogan, because I believe it's an anchor point of our faith and our future.

God... loves... you!

I need to hear this. You need to hear it. You need to know it. We are hard-wired by our Creator to love and be loved. In fact, as it so clearly states in the *Catechism of the Catholic Church*:

The desire for God is written in the human heart, because

man is created by God and for God; and God never ceases to draw man to Himself. Only in God will he find the truth and happiness he never stops searching for: the dignity of man rests above all on the fact that he is called to communion with God.[5]

All the junk that life has thrown our way seems to have blinded us to this supernatural truth, leaving us feeling like we have to be satisfied somehow with what we have. But that's simply not true. All of life has a meaning and a purpose. God, who knows us and deeply understands every single pain and burden, wants to use you and He wants to use me to show His love and His heart to a hurt and dying world. Through our pain, not despite it, He wants to use me and to use my family as mirrors that reflect Him, each and every day, to every soul we come across. He wants to use you too. But He wants us doing it from a place of knowing: knowing just who we are… loved by God, adorable and exquisite to Him.

Someone told me recently that we are just a blip on the landscape of history, that we have no right to think that we are any more than that. But that's wrong. Together, we are the bride of Christ. The bride is the focal point of the wedding day. People look at her and think: 'Whoa, who's the groom, that he gets her? Look how happy and in love she is.' The bride points to a groom, a man she's chosen to cast her entire life to, to join her identity to, to take his name, become his family. She is making a public statement that this man is worthy of her trust… to love and to cherish.

Well, that is what God is saying when He asks us to be the bride of Christ. He wants us looking all beautiful and gorgeous. He wants us to show the people of this world not all the stuff they're getting wrong but, instead, just how much He wants them, like a groom wants his wife.

And He's asking me; He is asking my family; He is asking you.

I'll never forget when a Māori (indigenous New Zealander) elder explained to me just how important it is for a man to know who he is and where he has come from. Every Māori can tell you the names of their family's mountain, river and sea; they can tell you their tribe's name, their father's name, their grandfather's name; and they can tell you who the founding chief of their tribe was. They *know* who they are. They know the history of their land... its trees, its battlegrounds, its sacred places. And they teach it to their children.

They know it and make it a priority to know it because it is their identity. The same applies to the Jews. They pass their Jewishness from mother to daughter. And I'm sure that it's the same for indigenous tribes and peoples the world over.

That discovery has led me to think that, generally speaking, we Christians don't know who we are. We don't know just how loved and precious we are. And equally as important, we don't see that the impact of our past has shaped who we are today, and it has shaped us for good. Unfortunately, we seem to have developed a misleading view of what God wants to reveal to the world. We've somehow fallen into the trap of thinking that we have to show them an artificial beauty. But, for me anyway, I figured that it was completely impossible to live up to the fake smile I have plastered on to my good Christian face... going through life, flashing our porcelain veneer-covered smiles, hoping no one notices the rot or pain behind them.

God says that unless I turn my heart back to the past, it will forever curse me and forever rob me of the future that He has in store for me. My father's narcissism, for example, impacted me in ways I just could not see; I have since learned that it actually caused me to hobble with insecurity… that ironclad vice of insecurity became a weight that I foisted onto my wife, my kids. But with the help of caring friends, a very wise counsellor and an exquisitely gentle God who loves me so very much, I am starting to trek back into my past and re-look at those cuts, those bruises and those scars.

God has called me to look back into my past – not to camp there or to live there, but to *look* back. He wants me to do this because that is where I have come from. It is part of the tapestry of who I am: the fabric of my story. I can't change a single thing of my past, but God is changing how I see it. And that, I know, is changing me and making me free. The pain may always be there to some degree, but the grip of the curse that bleeds me is not.

God marks

I see that I am worthy of something – I am worth God's extreme love. And that discovery is helping to change the way that I look at the puncture marks in my life lived so far, so I see them not as scars, but as *God marks.*

God wants to take our lives and make them things of beauty… no, He already has made them things of beauty; it's just that we can't seem to see it. People who know more than I do about this kind of thing tell me that the true quality of a rug is actually what's underneath: the knots. The closer together they are, the better the rug. The rug of God, that every person created has been woven into, is something of exquisite beauty – He has been weaving for thousands of years. The only problem is that when I look up at it, all I seem to see is an awful lot of knots. And they are tight and ever so close together. That's the difficulty that we seem to have with our pain; we see only the knots of pain and evil in our lives. What incredible joy we'll have when God allows us the luxury of looking down on this thing to see only beauty. It's with tears that I write this – God sees all our pains, all our faults and all our humanity together as a very deliberate picture of beauty. He sees you and me, and says that we are part of something divinely beautiful.

If that is, in fact, true and not just a nice picture I've dreamed up in my own head, if this life is actually ordered by God for our good, if the knots and the struggles are somehow part of His ordering of our steps, how are we to make it through? If we are drowning with the weight of the pain of it, where is the answer? Where is the hope?

Malachi 4:6 tells us that Elijah is coming back and he's going to turn the hearts of fathers to their children and, also, he's going to turn the hearts of children to their fathers. Through the prophet Malachi, God is letting us know that He earnestly desires for the hearts of fathers to be turned to their children and for the hearts of those children to be turned to their fathers.

The picture I have when I read these words is that of a flower leaning into the sun. It infers a desire to be near, to want to be with. And who are the fathers referred to here in the last few pages of the Old Testament of the Bible anyway? Does God really expect you and me to take this notion literally and apply it to our own lives? I have heard a lot about the importance of the first part of that verse, but I don't recall ever hearing about the second part. Yet hidden here is the clue to so many of the mountains we face in our own lives. In all my years working for family-help organisations, I have discovered that so many people, including far too many Christians (I'm on that list too!), have skeletons in the closet. Whether it's through a distorted theology, shame or sheer survival, we have somehow lost sight of the blazing power of the cross of Christ to bring healing to our past. Instead of us laying our cares at the foot of the cross, that Holy Tree has become a dumping ground where we hide the pains of our past. And then (the picture is almost comical, if it weren't so painfully true), instead of sitting at His feet with all those issues and working through them *with Him*, we dump them and run as far from any reminder of that past as is humanly possible.

Do you get the irony here? In our desperation to run from all that, we also run from the one place where true, genuine healing comes from.

God has made it very clear that this isn't what He wants. He wants us to shine the light of truth onto those areas in our lives that seem to be always trying to drag us down. He wants us to turn and look at who we are, He wants us to turn and look at where we have come from, and He wants us to turn and look into the eyes of the people who took us, or who may have dragged us, there. God wants us to understand that these things and these people have shaped us; they are the founding pillars, the founding fathers in our lives. We are who we are because of them. No matter how you repaint the walls, your house is still your house. It's the same with your life – your past is part of the foundation of who you are today. If we don't find a way to see each and every part of our lives as something of which God is somehow a part, we will forever live as if our lives are a curse and not a blessing.

I'm sorry for your hurt and your pain, I really am. But we have to pick up that cross and follow Him; follow him back to Calvary, where our pasts are waiting to be dealt with.

Drawing from the wisdom of the Desert Fathers, those ancient Christian hermits, ascetics, and monks who lived mainly in the deserts of Egypt around the third century AD and whose wisdom profoundly influenced the development of Christianity, John

Chryssavgis put it this way: 'you do not have to find the desert in your life; it normally catches up with you … If we go through this experience involuntarily, then it can be both overwhelming and crushing. If, however, we accept to undergo this experience voluntarily, then it can prove both constructive and liberating.'[6]

You might have come to this day weighed down with desperation and hopelessness, but 'despite life's many sorrows and sufferings,' as Christopher West says:

God does indeed have a perfect plan for our satisfaction. Let that lift you up. Let it fire you up. Let it give you hope. You're not crazy. You're not wrong to believe there's something more. You will not be unhappy. Have faith. Trust. Be open to the gift. It's coming. Your desire for Life is not in vain.[7]

Take Time

• Do you feel like you are drowning with the weight of the pain of your hurt… that there's no hope for you? Take some time to meditate on this thought:

The desire for God is written in the human heart, because man is created by God and for God; and God never ceases to draw man to Himself. Only in God will he find the truth and happiness he never stops searching for: the dignity of man rests above all on the fact that he is called to communion with God.[8]

• How do you feel about the idea that God causes all things to work for our good? What are the areas in your life where you can't see God's hand or His love? Do you think you can ask God to change how you see them, that you may know that your agony and damage is, in fact, part of something divinely beautiful?

Spend as much time as you need before moving on from here. It's not a sprint to the next chapter and anyway, God has plenty of time to help you navigate through it.

Pray

Oh God in heaven, help me right now to learn all I need to find my way into Your arms. Help me to see the bigger picture in the tapestry You are weaving my life into, and to see that my scars are beautiful to You. Help me, God, to see how You want to use my past and my pain for my good. God, I am scared, but I give it all to You, that I would see all of my life as a gift from You.

Amen.

Chapter Four:
What I Cannot Do

What I cannot do myself, Jesus will do.
He will take me and lift me up.[1]
St Therese of Lisieux

I just love the scene at the end of Darren Aronofsky's 2014 movie adaption of the account of Noah and the great flood, where a very hungover and forlorn Noah (played by Russell Crowe) is seen sitting on a rock wallowing in self-pity. He was depressed because he felt that he'd somehow failed his Creator – he couldn't bring himself to slaughter his new-born granddaughters. In his mind, it was to be the defining act of this last man, in what he felt was God's final solution for a humanity beyond redemption.

I know there are plenty of people upset about how this movie attempted to portray the biblical narrative. Whatever the thoughts are on the theology of Hollywood's painting of this biblical story, I actually think that it did a really brilliant job of challenging us on how we deal with personal pain. Noah, who was a man of unshakeable vision and purpose, had sadly become so intensely caught up in setting up protective walls from the dangers he knew hid in the darkness, that he lost sight of his calling. And as he turned more and more inward in search of the *real meaning* of that vision, the voice and guidance of the Vision-giver grew more and more dim.

Noah, in this movie, turned completely away from God's call for him to build a safe place for those set apart for God's future plans. Instead, Noah started to believe his own confused view of this and ended up building an entirely different ark. He shut out the people in his life, and tried even harder to find some way to make sense of what was going on around him. Problem was, he was using the faulty wisdom of human reasoning.

I can see how he did this. I continue to muddle my way through the ongoing wrench between what appears to be the irrationality of faith and trust in a God I can't see, while trying to exist, to raise my family, to live in a very rational world. It makes no sense to take my hands off the handlebars, especially when the ride is downhill. I think I act a lot like Aronofsky's Noah, taking my future into my own hands, building my own ark that will take me away from the very things that God has brought into my life.

Near the end of the film, Noah had become so convinced of his own internal god-speak that he sees the only way for God's plan to be fulfilled is by killing his own family. He couldn't bring himself to complete his final solution, and that threw him into a spiritual tailspin. He'd become so caught up in the destructive internal dialogue that Satan was able to sneak on board and steal what little hope he had left. Self-pity and lies cause us to fall into a cycle of poor choices – Noah's was the *genius* idea of drinking himself into oblivion, throwing hope away and turning his back on the very people God had called him to spend the best part of his life building the ark to save.

Dad let me down

Even though I had made it my goal to follow God and to strive for Him to be my role model of a father, and for Jesus to be my role model of a man, I still had a really hard time to not feel people in my life had failed me. Because Dad continually *let me down* in these areas, my internal voice told me that God wanted me to surround myself with people who would prove to me that it was possible to be a perfect godly man. I strived for that myself and to find it in everyone around me. If I followed God in this way, I'd never botch it and nor would the people God brought into my life. Time and again I'd fail to meet the spiritual expectations I'd built up for myself, and so would everyone else I laid the same weight of expectation on. My tailspin would send me into a dark, hopeless depression. My world would collapse around me. The lies would come pouring into the emptiness – God had failed me yet again; I'd failed Him. What's worse, like Noah, because I had been drawn by the whispers and lies, I had come to believe that I had a right to my pain because of the rubbish of my past.

The real beauty of this whole scene in the movie is when Shem's wife comes to Noah and talks to him about his brokenness. She tells him that the Creator knew him and chose him because He knew Noah's heart. God knew that Noah, despite his broken humanity, would make the right choice in the end. Even though he couldn't see it himself, Noah had made the right choice because God had wired him to make the right choice. God knew what Noah needed to go *through* in order to shape him and make him into the founding father of the new world. And that is also true of each of us.

This is one of the hardest chapters for me to write; the words you are about to read and the thoughts I want us to chew over are hard to swallow. I have agonised over how to write them in a way that won't cause you to shut off and miss out on what is coming. This chapter will bring with it some pain, but just as the restoration of a precious painting needs tireless patience, peeling, scratching and scraping, so we need to let the hand of the Master Painter go to work on our lives, cleaning and restoring the masterpiece that is us. In saying all that, I don't want to minimise your pain and I definitely don't want to be flippant about the people who have hurt you.

When we live under the assumption that our past has the power to butcher us and wreck our future, it causes our rational mind to see faith and trust in God as irrational. Yet God calls us to step out of the boat and believe that the Bible is truth, that all things will work for our good. God wants room to shine the light of truth in and on you, so as carefully and as gently as I possibly can, I want to ask you to look at your own story. And as you allow the Spirit of God to wash away all the cover-up and grime, I pray that you'll be able to ask yourself if you really do have a right to your pain and your pity.

That's tough, right? What's even tougher is that once we start looking back at our past in this way, we then need to find the strength to take a step forward, and then another and another. We need to walk in God's strength and we need to trust in Him as He reveals the good that He had in mind, allowing us to endure such things.

I know that there is sin in the world and that sin makes others do terrible things. I know that virtually every one of us is living proof of that. And I know that the pain is real and that the damage is genuine. If you're anything like me, you have prayed, you have fasted, you have pleaded and you have screamed, and yet you just can't shake the agony of the past. But God teaches that we have no right to claim our pain as an excuse to live broken. The time has come for us to let God take our suffering and transform it. But don't be overwhelmed, He'll send a *Shem's wife* to you too, to remind you that God knew what you needed to go *through* in order to shape you. Use this time to learn to listen and to hear what the Lord God is saying to you.

Hate the sickness

There is so much richness to be found in the ancient writings of the Desert Fathers and Mothers. As you sift through it, there are beautiful nuggets that seem timeless in their sagacity. Syncletica of Alexandria lived in the fourth century and was said to have given away her considerable fortunes to the poor, to live out her days in a cave in the Egyptian desert. According to John Chryssavgis' *In the Heart of the Desert*, when asked about how to deal with unforgiveness, she replied: 'Why hate the person who has harmed you? It is not the person who has done the wrong. Hate the sickness, but do not hate the sick person.'[2]

I love that statement, *on paper*. In reality, I first read it and questioned how some crazy woman who ran off to the desert to deal with her problems, could somehow cure my demons with a flippant brush-off in response to the punishment of the people who had damaged my soul.

But the more I ponder that sort of teaching and the more I sit with it, the more I let it sink deeper into my own experiences and the more I let the idea weigh on my thoughts and my mind, and most importantly, as I let the words into my broken heart, I see God asking me to turn my heart over to Him. When we choose to hold onto our resentment, we will always suffer from the bitterness of the soul. While we continue to consciously or unconsciously store unforgiveness in our hearts, we will live with the curse of what Satan meant as harm, blinded to the fact that God intends to use it for good.

As we go through the agonising process of *letting go and letting God*, we are slowly being made free... every day an opportunity to let go a little more, allowing a little more of God in. That freedom is like gasoline that fuels God's plans to give you hope and a future![3]

I haven't met a person yet who managed to find the secret formula that wipes their mind of that sort of past. Forgiveness doesn't mean that we are going to have to invite the person we have forgiven over for Christmas dinner. We may never reach a place where we can even say the name of the person. God's drawing and leading us to a place where we can choose to forgive does not somehow imply that God is in any way OK with the pain-maker. And it definitely doesn't mean that we turn a blind eye to anyone who continues to do harm. Sin is *never* OK; neither is choosing not to act when sin is being perpetrated. 'The truest obedience to God is the opposition to tyranny'.[4]

But unless you somehow find a way to cast off the enormous burden that comes with holding on to a past that may have been pushed upon you, you will forever be a slave to it… it will cloud the way you view everything and everyone. When he was battling with his own issues of unforgiveness, theologian R.T. Kendall felt God whisper: 'RT, you must totally forgive them. Until you totally forgive them, you will be in chains. Release them and you will be released.'[5] He went on to echo the words written by Syncletica of Alexandria, 1,700 years earlier. In his book *Total Forgiveness*, Kendall says, 'I should not hold people responsible for what they have done to me. I will hold nothing against them …'[6]

He chose to hold nothing against the people who had hurt him so deeply. He actually went on to say that he would never even speak of it to others, either. How is it that we are expected to let go completely, when the damage has come at such a huge cost to us and has sent ripples through the rest of our lives? That is such a fair question. But the answer is equally plain:

Jesus says: 'Follow me…'

Live with the glimpse of heaven

He didn't wait for repentance on the part of His enemies before He called out to heaven in His misery: 'Father, forgive them …'[7] Through that single act, Jesus made heaven wholly and freely available to us. The absolute heartbreak of that utterly profound concept is that too often we don't live with the glimpse of heaven that God gave us when He ripped the veil from the Temple that day.[8] Instead, we have turned the other way, with a full-on view of hell.

While the principles are steadfast, the footsteps we take to follow them are completely individual and unique. Each of us must search for our own way of coming to terms with these truths, unafraid to seek, to search and to try… even at the risk of getting it wrong, sometimes, along the way. We must find some way to follow in the dust of our great Teacher so that we too can, through our suffering, sit in the presence of God. If we don't choose to turn our hearts back in forgiveness, we choose Malachi's curse on our land, and in doing that we continue to deny the fullest power of God in and through each part of our lives.

I was talking with my mum about this and how it applied to her life. She stayed with my dad through so much. And for her, her biggest shame still is that maybe she was too weak to leave, too scared to go it alone. She had somehow grown to believe that she was such a victim that she couldn't find a way to live without this man who constantly caused her huge amounts of pain. But when we looked at her life, in light of Aronofsky's Noah, it created a very different story for her… she had a glimpse of herself as God sees her. She had made choices that God knew she would make: that were for her ultimate good. As she, like Nelson Mandela, found a way to look back from where her life had brought her, she saw that, in fact, the days she had felt she could endure no more, the days where her tears inked her already heavy heart, were not dark days at all, for they shone with the golden threads that God was using to weave her life's tapestry – those toughest of days were producing the gold that is now threaded all through her life, creating the most exquisite masterpiece.

My mum is one of the most incredible women you could ever meet. She has such a deep care and compassion for others, yet she would tell you herself that she would never have been the person she is today without the past that God has painstakingly used to shape her.

St Augustine tells of how hard it was for Monica, his mother, when he left home to travel to Rome. Apparently she thought this would be the ruining of him, given that he was already spending far too much time with a group of young men who openly boasted of their sexual conquests with both women and men.

While sailing to Rome, he prayed:

Why I left the one country and went to the other, You knew, O God, but You did not tell either me or my mother. She indeed was in dreadful grief at my going; she remained praying and weeping. And what was she praying for, O my God, with all those tears but that You should not allow me to sail! But you saw deeper and granted the essential part of her prayer; You did not do what she was at that moment asking, that You might do the thing she was always asking.[9]

Monica's daily prayer was for Augustine to have a personal encounter with the Creator of heaven and earth. As he sailed off into the sunset, she had no way of knowing that had he not gone to Rome, where he truly met God and was converted, her prayer may have gone unanswered.

But here is the bit where faith and trust come in – while for Monica it looked like the worst of times, in God's economy it was all part of the plan. My mum, as hard as it was to come to that place of being able to admit it out loud, would wholeheartedly agree.

While Monica's story might not even cast a shadow on the experiences you have been through, while it might not appear to carry with it the same tragedy that you might have to wake up with each morning, memories that continue to kill you just a little more every day, it was a very real torment to her soul. She couldn't see any way for God to weave her son's story into the tapestry of history in any sort of righteous way. And, like you may be right now, she was in utter anguish.[10] But just as He did not abandon Monica, God did not and will not abandon you; He will bring good out of your pain. If you will let Him, He will step into your life because, in the words of Pope Francis:

> He truly loves us, He is alive, He is mysteriously capable of intervening, He does not abandon us and He brings good out of evil by His power and His infinite creativity.[11]

'But Tim,' you scream, 'try living it out when every day your life is filled with so much darkness. You have no idea of the price I have had to pay!' There's a very good chance that that's true; the fishhooks of pain are still embedded into your back. And no matter what you do, you just can't forgive, can't get free from the hurt caused to you.

I love the way C.S. Lewis put it, as only he could, when he said, 'Everyone says forgiveness is a lovely idea, until they have something to forgive … And half of you already want to ask me, "I wonder how you'd feel about forgiving the Gestapo if you were a Pole or a Jew?" So do I. I wonder very much.'[12]

Yet despite his personal struggle, he went on to say, 'There is no slightest suggestion that we are offered forgiveness on any other terms. It is made perfectly clear that if we do not forgive we shall not be forgiven. There are no two ways about it. What are we to do?'[13]

What are we to do? Well, as far as I can see it, no matter if we want to or not, or if we feel that we need to or not, or even if we think we are actually capable of it, we must find a way to make peace with our past. We must find a way to forgive. I don't have an easy one-size-fits-all answer. What I can tell you is that I have said no to God's idea of healing too many times to remember, but (The Message version of the Bible captures this beautifully) He always finds a way to remind me that He 'didn't go to all the trouble of sending his Son merely to point an accusing finger, telling the world how bad it was. He came to help'.[14]

This is the great love of God:

He came to help – He came to *help* – HE CAME TO HELP.

Take Time

- What is it that you find the hardest to do, the hardest to deal with? What are the points of pain that you just can't shift? Write them down or speak them out loud… put them out there!
- As you look at them, can you see what faulty reasoning and lies are attached to them?
- Can you see how they have shaped your choices or distorted God's reality for you?
- Remember the opening quote from St Therese of Lisieux, that 'What I cannot do myself, Jesus will do. He will take me and lift me up'.[15] I'd encourage you to take your time here and let Jesus

do some *doing.* Ask Him to help you see, hear and believe the words of Pope Francis as a personal truth: 'He truly loves us, He is alive, He is mysteriously capable of intervening, He does not abandon us and He brings good out of evil by His power and His infinite creativity.'[16]

Pray

This is a huge piece of the puzzle to process, so I'd like for you to do something you may never have done before in prayer: 'When the time comes and we cannot pray, it is very simple – let Jesus pray in us to the Father in the silence of our hearts. If we cannot speak, He will speak. If we cannot pray, He will pray. So let us give Him our inability and our nothingness.'[17]

Take some time to sit in the presence of God and give Jesus your nothingness and inability. Let him pray for what needs to be done in your life right now, for He came to help.[18]

Chapter Five:
The *Why* to Live For

He who has a *why* to live for can bear almost any *how*.[1]
Friedrich Nietzsche

What I'm discovering, as I research and write, is just how much God, the Creator of the entire universe, loves us. He loves us so overwhelmingly, so overabundantly, so overextravagantly, and then some! My bad English here goes to explain how hard it is for me to articulately and accurately sum that thought up with *actual* words. He loves us so much that He came to where we are, with the express purpose of giving us life. God cleared the bank account, so to speak, and invested the entire family savings into each one of us because He wants us to have it all, to live free from the shackles of our past. God looks down and smiles and He speaks words of life into our dead parts.

So even if paralysing grief is sapping you of strength to even inch forward, remember the words of the apostle John, that Christ came to help.[2] He has an answer for you – no, He has the answer. All we really have to do is find a way to let God in, to let Him bring His healing Spirit into the dark cellar of our hopelessness. It's with His help that we can learn to see that answer in our own experiences and in our own walk.

In the words of John Newton, 'with Christ in the vessel, I smile at the storm'.[3] But without Him in it, and I *really* believe this, there'll be no peace, no hope and ultimately no forgiveness. Instead, as it says in that last verse of Malachi, we will live under a curse.[4]

You may not feel the love you need in order to love the pain-maker in your life just yet, but fear not, for Jesus is right here with you, to help you. He whispers, 'I love you! Follow Me, mirror Me; I gave My everything for your sake. Follow Me; I love without limit or expectation, so follow Me. I am the best way, the right way… I am *the way.*' God is for you, and He has chosen to show you just how much He is for you and how much He loves you, through the pain caused to you. So go now, in His good grace and may the peace of God comfort your weary soul.

As hard as it might be to do, we need to be like the jewel merchant that Jesus spoke of in Matthew 13:45. He was 'on the hunt for excellent pearls. Finding one that is flawless, he immediately sells everything and buys it'.[5] That's the message – do whatever it takes to find the holy hope. Have faith, for God is with you and He will bring you life, hope, a future, and a smile in the storm.

A story of hope

A year or so ago, I had the opportunity to go to Russia, to see one of the most famous paintings of one of my all-time favourite artists. The piece of work was Rembrandt's 'The Return of the Prodigal Son' and it's housed in the Hermitage Museum in St Petersburg. The city was both, in my opinion, extraordinarily exquisite, but also somewhat sad. And it's not at all surprising, when you look at its recent history.

Almost half of the 70 million lives lost during the Second World War were somewhere along the massive Eastern Front. The conditions faced by the men and women (civilians and soldiers alike) were considered some of the most atrocious and hideous of any war in this planet's history. The horror that so many had to live through (and, inevitably, died experiencing) is sickening.

When the Nazi war machine finally reached the city of Leningrad (now St Petersburg), its citizens had no way of knowing what lay ahead of them – the now-infamous 900-day Siege of Leningrad. Infrastructure was completely wiped out. They had no power, no heating, water mains were frozen solid. Food was so scarce and the people so starved, regular mums and dads just like you and me were eating sawdust, cardboard, dirt, and much, much worse. By the time the siege was broken, according to original BBC news reports from January 1944, 'hundreds of thousands of Leningrad's population of 2.5 million [had] died of starvation, exposure, disease or enemy action'.[6]

No one was left untouched or unaffected. Twenty-five per cent of all the men, the women and the children of that proud city perished. Most of the human souls who had managed to somehow survive were left emotionally, physically and spiritually shattered.

Daniil Alexandrovich Granin compiled a book sharing first-hand accounts from survivors of the ordeal. It is chilling reading, but it's important to share some of the thoughts of those who found a way out of that bleak darkness. I'll explain why in a moment.

29 October 1941. I am now so weak that I can hardly make my legs work, and climbing the stairs is a huge effort for me … This nightmare, this horror, would surely have to end sometime. I can't stand it any longer – What gloomy thoughts are creeping into my brain! … It is becoming hard to go on living. To go

on living, not knowing what for, to go on living, dragging out your existence in hunger and cold … Each day that I live through here is a day that brings me closer to suicide. There is really no way out. It's a dead end, I can't go on living like this any longer … It is not difficult to die, but it is extremely hard to be dying … How agonizing this is! I am sitting here crying. I'm only sixteen years old, you know![7]

Yet, after almost 900 days of utter hopelessness and depravation, the Russians broke though the German lines and ended that death-siege. Those who survived, did so because they found a way:

Why such sad thoughts, so much melancholy? Since we have been given life, this priceless gift of nature, why should we dwell on its bad aspects? Think only of the good things of life, take from it all the pleasures that it has to give. Why waste it? … I so passionately want to live, to believe, to feel … we will endure, provided we don't lose the will to overcome obstacles.[8]

Their enduring to the end was because they had something that fed them to go on. As Daniil Alexandrovich Granin wrote, 'everyone is nourished by hope'. They had hope that something better was coming their way. They realised that 'Only someone who has lived through great sorrow, great suffering, can appreciate to its full extent the kind of happiness that exists only here on earth'.[9]

But the problem is that no one in their right mind likes pain. It's why we generally run from it rather than embrace it. I love how Steve Brown put it in his book, *A Scandalous Freedom*. He says:

That is also why we aren't free. Jesus hardly ever goes to those places where we run. When pain comes (or when we fear that it will come), don't run away. Run to it, and you will find you have run into the arms of Jesus … Then you will laugh and dance in the freedom and the reality of God's sufficiency and the power that becomes awesome in your weakness.[10]

Don't lose heart and don't lose hope. Instead, ask God to give you faith to push on, because He will 'heal the brokenhearted … provide for those who mourn [with] a crown of beauty instead of ashes, festive oil instead of mourning, and splendid clothes instead of despair'.[11]

Learn from others

The early Church used the term Eucharist (from the Greek word εὐχαριστία or Eucharistia) when referring to Communion. The word is actually really important, because it translates into our English word 'Thanksgiving' – an opportunity to bring God into our lives and thank Him for it all. The American celebration of Thanksgiving is, in fact (despite its commercialisation), a nationwide Eucharist or Communion! According to the Coptic tradition, the Eucharist allows us to become partakers of the Divine Nature and is a medicine or tonic to the soul, body and spirit. The Orthodox traditions suggest that this Thanksgiving is literally feeding on Christ… Christ who sustains us as we go through our week.

I've read hundreds of stories and biographies of people who, over the centuries, have been thrust into the type of pain or horror that only exists in the recesses of terrifying nightmares. The theme that runs through all their stories is the same – they didn't lose hope. They all found something that gave them the strength and the insight to choose to thank God in and for their situation, no matter what they had been through or were facing. They discovered the incredible power and freedom that comes only through making the conscious decision to invite Him into their pain, to breathe Him in and to breathe out the poison of hate, anger and resentment.

St Ignatius describes this process as asking for the grace that all our intentions, actions and operations may be directed purely to the praise and service of the Divine Majesty.[12] I recently stumbled on a song that so beautifully echoes this. It moved me so much that I contacted the writer for permission to include it here, as a meditation for us, as we mull through and attempt to process all of this:

Breathe, breathe on me now;
Open your mouth;
And speak the word that heals this broken ground
Say, say what You will;
Show us Your will;
As we breathe in the very breath of God
Oh, Spirit of God;
Here with us now, giving us life again;
Breathe, breathe on us now
Fill us with Your love;
Send us with Your power; Spirit of God
Oh, Spirit of God;
Here with us now, give in us life again;
Breathe, breathe on us now
Fill us with Your love;
Send us with Your power; Spirit of God
('Breathe' from the album *The Brilliance* by The Brilliance)[13]

Here's the thing – if you and I want to live, I mean really live, free of the constant dredging of the seafloor of our lives, if we want to truly experience what it feels like to have God's Spirit filling our lives, if we want the broken ground made fertile again, I am becoming more and more certain that we have to do everything we can to put ourselves in a place where we are actually capable of choosing this day whom we will serve… will it be the hate, the hurt, the hunger for justice and fairness? Or will you, will I, choose this day to let God be the lamp to our feet and the light to our path?[14]

With the slight fear that I might shut you down, I want to speak plainly: You and I, we have a choice to make every single day. And that choice is to choose to live like a pig in the squalor and slop, or, like the prodigal son, we can choose to go to the Father and let Him wrap us in a new robe.

After surviving the massacres of Rwanda, Immaculée Ilibagiza painted the most beautiful picture of this. She said:

> I came to learn that God never shows us something we aren't ready to understand. Instead, He lets us see what we need to see, when we need to see it. He'll wait until our eyes and hearts are open to Him, and then when we're ready, He will plant our feet on the path that's best for us … but it's up to us to do the walking.[15]

I love that so much: 'He will plant our feet on the path that's best for us … but it's up to us to do the walking.'[16] That is from someone who has experienced first-hand the kinds of horrors that very few (God willing) will ever come close to experiencing. If you get the opportunity to read her book, I would encourage it. Her point is just so important to those of us grappling with a life still riddled with the bullet holes of our past. But the Bible is clear, Jesus is clear. He tells us to pray that God might forgive us to the same degree that we forgive others. What does that mean to you? Does it mean to no longer talk about it? Does it mean to no longer think about it? The answer is yes and yes, but even more, it means that before we bury it, we must deal with it, with God. He calls us to get a grip of the fact that nothing happens without it going through God's hand first.

Let that thought take root... because if that is true, then maybe the answer to the stumbling block of why bad things happen to good people is because God wills it. We see it in the biblical account of Job, where Satan has to get permission before he can do anything to harm or hurt Job. We also see it in the words of Christ, when He heals the blind man man in in John Chapter 9.[17] We hear it again in Immaculée Ilibagiza's story, and it reverberates throughout history, in the words of scores of others who have written about their own experiences of concentration camps, genocides, pogroms. But while we might hear it, it's pretty rare for any of us to choose to let it be our own truth in our own lives.

The Didache[18] is probably one of the earliest writings of the Christian Church, dated by most scholars to the first century after Christ, or early in the second century AD. It is a very short writing, but in its brevity, it is also very plain and clear – it teaches us this:

> Bless those who curse you, pray for your enemies, fast for those who persecute you. Accept whatever happens to you as good, knowing that apart from God nothing comes to pass.[19]

In terms of this particular statement, I get that it might be too hard to accept just now. I've chewed and chewed on it and I still find it tough to swallow. On the face of it, for God to willingly cause harm appears to bring Him down to the level of Satan. And that is why, for most Christians, we have settled on the route that instead, God sometimes allows harm because He has a bigger plan that we will one day see. But how is that any less unloving and uncaring – a God who can do all things sets up a system that blocks Him from protecting us from pain and tragedy?

My hope is in a perfect, loving Father who always has the best interests of His children at the centre of His motivation. I have hope that God sees what I need to go through to get to the place where I can fully experience His love for me. I have hope that it's His will for me to carry this cross, because ultimately it's for my very best.

Take Time

- Let's take some time to process what we've just read. We started this chapter looking at God's overflowing love for us, and finished with a statement that more people have struggled with than anything else I talk about in this book – our pain is part of God's will for us *because* He loves us.
- So how does that make you feel? If it's just too hard to swallow, don't swallow it! Instead, remember that Christ has already made a way… sit with Him and commune with Him over it. When we feed on Christ and with Christ, we are nourished by divine hope.
- Thinking now about the statement that 'everyone is nourished by hope'… what tangible ways do you need nourishing, so you'll have the strength to run towards your pain, knowing Christ is there with His arms wide open?

Pray

Dear loving Father,

Thank You that You love me so deeply. Help me to have a heart that is nourished by divine hope. I pray that You would bless those who have cursed me. I pray for my enemies and for those who have and who continue to persecute me. God, I declare that, apart from You, nothing comes to pass. Teach me how to accept that whatever has happened to me is Your will and it is somehow good. Please be gracious with me as I choose daily this way, Your way. Breathe on me now; open your mouth; speak the word that will heal this broken ground.[20]

> Begone, unbelief; my Savior is near, and for my relief will surely appear; though dark be my way, since he is my guide, 'tis mine to obey, 'tis his to provide; though cisterns be broken and creatures all fail, the word he has spoken shall surely prevail. Since all that I meet shall work for my good, the bitter is sweet, the med'cine is food; though painful at present, with Christ in the vessel, I smile at the storm.[21]

Amen.

Chapter Six:
You'll Enjoy Heaven That Much More

*If you go through a little hell now
you'll enjoy heaven that much more.*[1]
Beaufort (a novel)

When I sat down to write a book about dealing with the pain in my life, I started out with the intention of seeking and finding *the* answer … I know that ultimately Jesus is all we need, but what I wanted was the tangible answer that would enable me to *tap into Jesus* every time I needed and every time I hurt. I felt certain that there was some sort of master key that would unlock the universal door of hope. If I did discover that key, I could've opened the door for all of us. And I wanted that – to hand you hope, all packaged up in ten nice, neat little chapters of answers. It would have been even more perfect if I could've woven in a whole lot of rocky stories from my own profound breakthrough experiences, and then when you turned the final page, all the pain would somehow magically drift away like the lifting fog on an autumn morning. You would be able to join me on the other side of the river of our pain and free of the ones who hurt us. We'd have the sun on our backs and our happy future set before us.

If I could have written such a book, I would have. I desperately wanted to latch on to something that oozed hope and healing and freedom from all that is horrible and sad in my life. And I wanted to be able to take that and put it in your hands too.

But the more I searched for God's silver bullet on this issue, the more I hit what appeared to be dead end after dead end. No matter which way I turned, I just couldn't find that elusive secret passageway that would lead us to the storehouse of heaven where we could drink freely of the miraculous fountain of amnesia, where we could be washed clean of the foul stink that our past has left us with.

No matter how hard I tried to find another way, an easier way, each of those dead ends seemed to bring me back to the same conclusion: You are who you are today, having been through all that you have been through, because *God Wills It*.

As I'm sure you can imagine, this one issue has probably consumed me more than any other part of this book. I have agonised over how to write this chapter, rolling the questions around in my mind. I have been on my knees over this for ages. How can it be that God would somehow *will* the misery and heartbreak that has so shaped my life, shaped yours, shaped all of history?

I *get* that God loves me and cares for me. I get that He will come through for me, somehow, in the end. Although the best example of this that I could come up with, short of the few miracles we see today (compared to what we read about in Scripture), is that it is in death that we will ultimately find freedom. If you go through a little hell now, 'you'll enjoy heaven that much more'.[2] But that is not really the hope-filled answer that I've been searching for, to answer the question of '*why*?' in the face of all the human struggles of the world. Nor does it come close to adequately answering that same question for you or me, at a personal level.

Don't run from suffering

I looked at all that I have been through and I've argued with God about how all of that could have been necessary for my good and my growth. Surely He could have come up with a better, less painful alternative. And Jesus gets that struggle; He had the very same conversation in Gethsemane, when He sweated drops of blood and cried out, 'Father, you can – can't you? – get me out of this. Take this cup away from me.'[3]

I wanted to run as far away from that possibility as I could, but it was a king hit. It took my feet out from under me. And as I hit the ground with the weight of this heavy in my heart, Jesus whispered the rest of that verse into my heart, 'But please, not what I want – what do you want?' He started to reveal to me the truth of this life that we live – that:

Anyone who intends to come with me has to let me lead. You're not in the driver's seat – I am. Don't run from suffering; embrace it. Follow me and I'll show you how. Self-help is no help at all. Self-sacrifice is the way, my way, to finding yourself, your true self. What good would it do to get everything you want and lose you, the real you?[4]

The Holman Christian Standard Bible expresses those words this way: 'If anyone wants to come with Me, he must deny himself, take up his cross daily …'[5]

I know we say it, pray it and sing it all the time, but I see now that this life actually involves the agony of a holy cross; that we each must choose to take up that cross and follow the footsteps of Christ; that God, for reasons I'm not sure we'll ever fully understand this side of heaven, wills it.

God wills it, for the good of those who love Him.

He knows us far better than we know ourselves, knows our pregnant condition, and keeps us present before God. That's why we can be so sure that every detail in our lives of love for God is worked into something good. God knew what he was doing from the very beginning. He decided from the outset to shape the lives of those who love him along the same lines as the life of his Son. The Son stands first in the line of humanity he restored. We see the original and intended shape of our lives there in him.[6]

So here's the truth – if the great and marvellous Architect of heaven and earth, whose ultimate act of love for each one of us was the excruciating pain that Jesus endured through the spikes, thorns and splinters of the cross, *wills it*, then we also must believe and reconcile ourselves to the fact that there has to be love behind every bit of pain and distress we have experienced. We must fix our eyes on the Creator of truth and figure out how to run into His arms. And that short, yet perhaps gruelling run, is unique for each one of us; it's not a one-size-fits-all approach, because just as our God loves us and sees us all as individuals, He has worked it so that we each have our own personal journey of discovery.

As I am starting to see for myself, if we don't choose to go through that process and come to the place where we can live with whatever burden and path God has chosen for us to experience or go through, the alternative is a curse... death of soul, death of body... death, death, death! These thoughts aren't new either, they live in the shadow of an ancient exchange between the God-Man, Jesus, and His disciples, when they asked Him, 'Rabbi, who sinned, this man or his parents, that he was born blind?'[7] We always manage to somehow forget the *man*. That man the apostles wanted to make a life lesson out of had spent a lifetime living in the dust of their shoes, and yet they missed the man, puffed out the chest and philosophised, trying to figure out who to tear strips off. And I find that all too often, we are not that different today – instead of seeing a beautiful soul made in the image of God, we see their sin and want to find out who and what went wrong!

But check out our Master's response – it was a complete jaw-dropper. According to John's Gospel, the Man despised and rejected by mankind, a man of suffering, and familiar with pain[8], says, 'Neither hath this man sinned, nor his parents: but that the works of God should be made manifest in him.'[9] Or in the language of Eugene Peterson and *The Message* Bible, 'You're asking the wrong question. You're looking for someone to blame. There is no such cause-effect here. Look instead for what God can do.'[10] Jesus makes it clear that this man's blindness, that had afflicted him since birth, was *an act of God* and part of the divine plan for his life. And if it was the case for him, why wouldn't it be the same for you and for me? It is time that we seek to accept that God made us who we are. I'm not suggesting that we embrace the struggle as an excuse to indulge in sin, Paul makes that very clear in Romans 6. Instead allow yourself to see your life, your struggles and your pain as part of who you are and part of what God has and is using to shape you… learn to look for what God can do *with* it.

God planned it for good

Going right back to the beginning of the human story, to the very first book of the Bible, we read these words: '*You* planned evil against me; *God* planned it for good to bring about the present result'.[11] Through the prophet Isaiah, God declares, 'I am the

LORD, and there is no other. I form the light and create darkness, I bring prosperity and create disaster; I, the LORD, do all these things.'[12]

The Bible tells us over and over and over again that God loves us so very, very much and yet that most sacred of Christian books seems to be constantly bringing us back to the reality that God also takes us by the hand and actually *leads* us down pathways of pain. And He does this so that He can bring us to the place where we can experience His loving presence in our lives.

This is a pretty tough pill to swallow. It just doesn't make sense to us in our humanness, in our hurt and broken reality. What are we meant to do with it? How do we reconcile our pain in the context of God's love for us?

And this conversation is by no means a new argument. Christians have been wading through this issue for centuries. I really like how Miroslav Volf so candidly expresses his inner turmoil in his search for somewhere to hang his hat on the matter, so to speak. He says:

> My thought was pulled in two different directions by the blood of the innocent crying out to God and by the blood of God's Lamb offered for the guilty. How does one remain loyal both to the demand of the oppressed for justice and to the gift of forgiveness that the Crucified offered to the perpetrators? I felt caught between two betrayals – the betrayal of the suffering, exploited, and excluded, and the betrayal of the very core of my faith. In a sense even more disturbingly, I felt that my very faith was at odds with itself, divided between the God who delivers the needy and the God who abandons the Crucified.[13]

I love the raw honesty of that statement. It expresses my feelings so aptly – how his faith was at odds with itself. God allowing pain and torment doesn't seem to make any sense at all… or, at least, that's the way it feels for me, anyway. But God is leading us to a place of understanding, and with that understanding and discovery of His *better way*, comes mind-blowing freedom.

God, in the midst

And I mean mind-blowing (because it's just too hard to get your head around!). Here it is – no longer do I need to try to figure out the why. I need to learn to live in the presence of God, in the *midst* of the anguish. This is the secret… there will always be pain. Human beings will go on hurting human beings. The body will break down. In my research for this book, I have read dozens of writers from across the denominations and from throughout the ages. God has whispered through the pages of their heartfelt struggles and utter anguish of soul, as they, like each of us, have wrestled with what to do with this realisation that God is the Master Craftsman of all things. These ageless writers have themselves agonised to find a way for this truth to come alive and to help us searchers and readers. They, too, desperately wanted to find some hint of the way around *God wills it*.

I gasped as I came to a place of actually being able to accept and admit out loud that God is behind and before; He is in and around; He is all-in-all. Nothing, not a thing, happens without it going across His desk first, nor without Him allowing it… *nothing*!

History is littered with experience after heart-tearing experience that prove this to be true. But in the words of my own mum: 'Once you managed to come through the smoke of the battle, you somehow realised that God actually got the path right. I can't explain it, I just know.' In the book of Proverbs,

Solomon (to whom God gave extraordinary wisdom and insight) tells us that in our heart we plan out our path, but *it is God* who determines the steps we take.[14]

Let's follow that thought through to its natural conclusion.

If the words of Solomon are true and to believed, then we have to find a way to come to grips with the reality that it is God who determines whether He will allow evil to affect our lives, and it is God who decides how that evil is to be used. We have to come to terms with, and make peace with, the reality that it is God who creates darkness and disaster, it is God who designs the road we will walk, with all the pitfalls and distractions along the way. Just as He told the prophet in Isaiah 45, He tells us now: 'I, the LORD, do all these things.'[15]

This does not diminish your pain, nor does it somehow attempt to absolve the actions and sins of others. God is very clear that what we do to others, we do to Christ Himself. Judgement is already prepared for the perpetrators of pain. But what it does help us see, as Solomon said in Proverbs 16, is that it is God who shines the light onto the road in front of us. I actually prefer the way that *The Message* puts it, for it speaks to us of hope: 'We plan the way we want to live, but only GOD makes us able to live it.'[16]

God wills it, God plans it, God determines the steps we take, but here is our hope – it is so important that this is not missed – it is also God who makes us able to live it! The fact is that Jesus made a promise in John 14:16. He promised each one of us that He would never ever leave us alone, but through His Spirit He would be our comfort and healer. In his book, *Finding God in All Things*, Brian Grogan writes, 'If someone asked you to give them another word for "God", you could use the word "Presence", for that is what God is. When Moses asked Yahweh his name, Yahweh replied, "I am who I am" and this means "I am present".'[17]

And that is what that verse in Isaiah 45 is telling us. It reminds us that God says, 'I am *for* you and I will *always* be there for you… yes, even to the end of time!'

If all of that is true, and I happen to think it is, then I also have to believe that what seems to us like a hopeless dead end, filled with nightmares and grief, is actually seen as something very different to the God who loves us so much. This truth is drawn out so incredibly beautifully in the words of Christ in the book of John, when in chapter 9 He says to His followers (and that's us too, by the way), 'You're looking at it all wrong. Instead, you need to look at what God can do with the situation that you are in (and not what could have been), at what He wants to do with you, to you, through the situation.'

So what do we do with that? Well, in the forty-second chapter of Job it says: 'After the LORD had finished speaking to Job, He said to Eliphaz the Temanite: "I am angry with you and your two friends, for you have not spoken the truth about Me, as My servant Job has."'[18] What's being revealed to us here is this – rather than searching out the right theological answers to somehow make the pain OK, Job goes to God and, with anguish of soul, he grapples with his grief directly with God Himself. It is Job's act of honesty and transparency that God honours.

If God is with you, and if God had a hand in the pain caused to each of us, and if that was for our good and our best, then just as Job did, we need to go to God. We need to go to Him and we need to ask Him to show us what He's actually capable of doing in and with our lives. God alone has the hope for our tired and weary souls; He alone has the faith we need to rise up and face this day. He is the Artist and we are the clay… let's give the Creator space and room to create.

Take Time

- We've bitten into some bitter fruit here, and like anything that's prickly and hard to swallow, there's a natural tendency to spit it out before we've had a chance to get any goodness from it. So as we take some time now, chew and meditate on the King David Psalm below. Think about the words that David prays and ask God to help you pray them – in light of your own situation and experiences. Be like Job who grappled with God over his grief – he discovered that what we see as darkness, is not necessarily darkness to God.

- You already know what you think and feel about your life, but now you need to ask God to pull the curtain back so you can see the *truth* that He sees when He looks at you. Journal if you need to; talk with others if that works; get on your knees; scream; cry; be silent… do whatever you need to do, but don't move past this point until you can make some sense, even if it's just a glimmer of light, of God's love and will for you in and through those experiences.

Pray

God, investigate my life;
get all the facts firsthand.
I'm an open book to you;
even from a distance, you know what I'm thinking.
You know when I leave and when I get back;
I'm never out of your sight.
You know everything I'm going to say
before I start the first sentence.

I look behind me and you're there,
then up ahead and you're there, too –
your reassuring presence, coming and going.
This is too much, too wonderful –
I can't take it all in!
Is there anyplace I can go to avoid your Spirit?
to be out of your sight?
If I climb to the sky, you're there!
If I go underground, you're there!
If I flew on morning's wings
to the far western horizon,
You'd find me in a minute –
you're already there waiting!
Then I said to myself, 'Oh, he even sees me in the dark!
At night I'm immersed in the light!'
It's a fact: darkness isn't dark to you;
night and day, darkness and light, they're all the same to you.
Oh yes, you shaped me first inside, then out;
you formed me in my mother's womb.
I thank you, High God – you're breathtaking!
Body and soul, I am marvelously made!
I worship in adoration – what a creation!
You know me inside and out,
you know every bone in my body;
You know exactly how I was made, bit by bit,
how I was sculpted from nothing into something.
Like an open book, you watched me grow from conception to
birth;
all the stages of my life were spread out before you,
The days of my life all prepared
before I'd even lived one day.

Your thoughts – how rare, how beautiful!
God, I'll never comprehend them!
I couldn't even begin to count them –
any more than I could count the sand of the sea.
Oh, let me rise in the morning and live always with you!
And ... guide me on the road to eternal life.[19]

Amen.

Part Two:
The Source of Hope

Chapter Seven:
He Came to Help

God didn't go to all the trouble of sending his Son merely to point an accusing finger, telling the world how bad it was. He came to help.[1]
John the apostle, the Bible

A few years ago now, when I was making the documentary *Irreplaceable*[2] for Focus on the Family, I had the opportunity to travel all over the world in search of some of the answers around the issues facing family today. Interestingly enough, it also became a personal journey of discovery for me too. I had the opportunity to talk with and interview some very wise people. It also put me in a lot of taxis, where I always seemed to have incredibly profound conversations with the cabbies.

After a long week of filming in Rome I found myself in the back seat of yet another taxi heading towards yet another airport and the driver said, 'Why you in Roma?' I was tired and not much in the mood to talk, especially having to navigate the language barrier, but I decided to tell him anyway – I had come in search of answers, answers to fix my pain. 'It's a brave thing,' he said, 'to choose to look at pain and people who make pain. That takes more courage!' And that was it; that was the end of the conversation.

His words struck me and have stuck with me. To choose

to look at our pain, to go in search of it with the intention of dismantling its power in our life *takes more courage*, incredible courage. But it's also where the answers are and is therefore our next step. I know that this idea is almost too mind-boggling to comprehend ... to dredge it all up, so that you can give it to God and suggest that He, as the giver of all things, needs to enable you to not only make some sort of sense of it, but more than that, to actually help you learn how to embrace the ugliness as some sort of gift from Him.

It's time for us to figure out what God is up to in our lives *today*. You can't change the actions of others, nor can you go back in time to change the way you reacted to those actions. To insist on making the past touch the present is to force yourself into some sort of macabre nightmare, over and over again. Nothing you do can change a jot of it. All you end up doing is to keep the candles burning over the altar of that rotting corpse that is your past. It is dead, DEAD! Yet in reality, it has never had a proper burial, so its stench so easily becomes an idol in our lives; an idol that every bit of our future is built on and built around.

But, in our defence, it's no surprise that so many of us default to such a way of life. The task, especially when life so often and so easily drowns us in the bitter waters of despair, is often just too much. Even in the Bible, through the wisdom of Solomon, we see that, 'If people can't see what God is doing, they stumble all over themselves.' But the story doesn't end there; in the very same breath, Solomon goes on to say that 'when they attend to what he reveals, they are *most blessed*'.[3]

If we can't see what God is doing in our life, then we'll stumble over ourselves. But when we do what He has shown us to do, we will be *most blessed*.

So let's just do it... let's spend time attending to what He wants to reveal; let's listen to instruction, as the Holman Christian Standard Bible puts it, because that's where the blessing is, that's where happiness lives. As I have mentioned earlier, to try to make sense of my own situation and to learn from those who have gone before me on the rocky road of life, I read and researched dozens of stories of people and cultures from throughout the centuries. All, one way or another, faced devastating situations and all desperately sought to find hope in the bleakness of pain. The ones who came through blessed or *oh, so happy,* were the ones who discovered that, in the words of Pope Benedict XVI, 'The dark door of time, of the future, has been thrown open. The one who has hope lives differently; the one who hopes has been granted the gift of a new life.'[4]

I know it's hard; I know the pain is so *painfully* real! But life is waiting on the other side of that dark door. And that is worth every ounce of the hard graft that comes with these few difficult steps.

In his book, *Where Is God When It Hurts?*, Philip Yancey shares the thoughts from Dr Paul Brand, one of the world's foremost experts on leprosy, speaking on the subject of pain. He quoted him as saying: 'Pain – it's often seen as the great inhibitor, keeping us from happiness. But I see it as a giver of freedom … If you ever doubt that, visit a leprosarium and observe for yourself a world without pain.'[5] Or as novelist Madeline Sheehan penned it, 'Everything has beauty; Even the ugly; Especially the ugly; Because without ugly, there would be no beauty. Because without beauty, we would not survive our pain, our sorrow, and our suffering.'[6]

C.S. Lewis had an almost life-shattering crisis of faith as he watched his best friend and wife, Joy Davidman, wither and die of bone cancer. The personal, secret journal he kept during that time has since been published, it's called *The Problem of Pain*. In that book, C.S. Lewis talks about how this experience taught him that

> The human spirit will not even begin to try to surrender self-will as long as all seems to be well with it ... But pain insists upon being attended to. God whispers to us in our pleasures, speaks in our conscience, but shouts in our pain: it is His megaphone to rouse a deaf world.[7]

Author Ron Leshem caught the idea beautifully in his award-winning novel *Beaufort*, which is set in the final days of Israel's withdrawal from Lebanon in the year 2000. The main character, an Israeli soldier and the last commander of the historic Fort Beaufort in Southern Lebanon had just made it back into Israel after a brutal final attack by the Islamist militant group, Hezbollah. As he contemplates what he had just been through and as he thinks about the number of friends who lost their lives to protect and defend Israel's northern border, only to retreat and give back everything that they'd spent years dying and bleeding for, he says this:

> If peace doesn't come in the meantime, I want my own kid to go through what I did. The challenges, the pain, the fear. They made me look at the world in a different way, find myself and what's important to me. My love for my family and the love of my life, and how fragile they are. That's how it is when you're surrounded by people who have lost friends.[8]

James, who is widely believed to be the brother of Jesus and the Elder of the first church in Jerusalem, tells us to 'Consider it a great joy, my brothers, whenever you experience various trials, knowing that the testing of your faith produces endurance. But endurance must do its complete work, so that you may be mature and complete, lacking nothing'.[9]

The Message puts his words this way: 'Consider it a sheer gift, friends, when tests and challenges come at you from all sides … don't try to get out of anything prematurely. Let it do its work so you become mature and well-developed, not deficient in any way.'[10]

Whether they realised it or not, each one of them discovered a hidden treasure – that great joy or sheer gift James refers to. They discovered it in different ways, but each discovered it in exactly the same place – it lay hidden deep in the pain of their own circumstance… woven through their own affliction. It was a pearl of great price Jesus talks about in Matthew 13; it was life-giving hope.

In Saved by Hope, Pope Benedict XVI teaches that

'redemption' – salvation – is not simply a given. Redemption is offered to us in the sense that we have been given hope, trustworthy hope, by virtue of which we can face our present. The present, even if it is arduous, can be lived and accepted if it leads toward a goal, if we can be sure of this goal, and if this goal is great enough to justify the effort of the journey.[11]

It seems to me that the early Church understood that God used pain as a way to sculpt them, so that they would 'become mature and well-developed, not deficient in any way'. When Paul wrote to the persecuted Church of Rome, he reminded them not to be disappointed that God hadn't answered their prayers through the removing of tyranny. And instead, encouraged them with these words:

The difficult times of pain throughout the world are simply birth pangs. But it's not only around us; it's within us. The Spirit of God is arousing us within. We're also feeling the birth pangs. These sterile and barren bodies of ours are yearning for full deliverance. That is why waiting does not diminish us, any more than waiting diminishes a pregnant mother. We are enlarged in the waiting. We, of course, don't see what is enlarging us. But the longer we wait, the larger we become, and the more joyful our expectancy.[12]

Paul tells them that the pain they are going through is God's way of planting and growing hope within them. It is through this hope that we learn to live - the goal is most certainly great enough to justify the effort of this journey called life.

The most loving way

The Bible's heroes, and all those of faith who came after the writing of those holy pages, experienced the very things that we are discovering afresh today. And they remind us that we all go through pain and suffering in our lives because God sees that it is *the most loving way* that He knows to draw us closer to the hope we so desperately need in order to thrive as He has designed us to thrive!

I am so grateful to C.S. Lewis for the way that he tackled this overwhelming thought in *The Problem of Pain*. He stated that just because he was writing about it didn't mean that he had a complete handle on it. He wrote that the opposite was much closer to his reality, that he was the world's greatest coward when it came to pain. I would suggest that I might actually be in front of him, in the race away from life's burdens. But here's the simple truth, boiled down to as simple as I can make it – no matter how fast or how far you or I run, God is there; the Bible makes that truth crystal clear. In fact, Psalm 139 says that He's there before we even arrive. God is forever chasing us with the passion of a lover. And if God is there, then He is here right now too. God is right here experiencing every bit of our pain and suffering with us. It is through God's grace that we learn what it is we need to do to willingly accept and embrace our pain as part of our God-designed journey. I need to stress this, though – I'm not suggesting for one second that we wipe the blame or consequence from any human perpetrator of sin or suffering in our lives, as if they are somehow acting as the hand of God. What I am saying, however, is that if Christ, whose love for us is immeasurable and total, has allowed us to endure suffering for a season (however long that season happens to be), He has His reasons… reasons that are somehow for our ultimate benefit, and His desire is that we search for ourselves, that we would find the hidden treasure worth selling everything for - the God-breathed benefits and blessings.

I want to reiterate here that I don't understand why God has chosen to walk us through the valley of the shadow of death[13] in order to find such a hope, but it is becoming so clear to me that there is no way around this truth. And if there's no way around it, the question that needs be answered is this: 'What are we to do now?' If God has designed the human condition in such a way that it is from suffering we are healed, where is our relief?

Arthur Kleinman writes that 'amidst great danger and huge uncertainty, hope is what makes the human condition liveable'.[14] And perhaps it is that faith, the kind of hope-filled faith that held the early Church together in the face of insurmountable persecution. And if it worked for them, maybe there's something in it for us here today. They knew that it's in God, and in God alone, that we must choose to find this hope.

The early Church also teaches us that He did not give us this life-sized challenge and then just expect us to deal with it alone. As we saw above, the Gospel of John tells us that 'God didn't go to all the trouble of sending his Son merely to point an accusing finger, telling the world how bad it was. He came to help'.[15] God, in the person of Jesus Christ, stepped into the muck, filth and pain of our busted-up humanity. And He did this for the express purpose of saving us… to personally help us capture that illusive hope; He came that we might find *the way* to unearth the one thing that will enable us to live differently – to grow in hope and to find meaning and purpose in our past. It is Jesus alone who holds the keys to unlocking this faith-based, hope-filled life. He was the lifeline of the early Church; He was the sustenance that they required to endure such terrifying persecution; and He is the same for us today.

But as C. Baxter Kruger put it, in his brilliant little book, *Jesus and the Undoing of Adam*:

> We cannot live on the joy of our ancestors' discovery of Jesus. We must come to know him for ourselves. Each generation must seek him and find him. Only then will we experience the quickening and the life and freedom that our souls crave. Herein lies the crisis point for each generation in the Church.[16]

The essence of this statement is what makes Christianity unique. You can't simply be born into it and you can't sit back and live off another's experiences; each one of us must know Jesus for ourselves. The setting free that comes through Him comes through a personal knowing of Him. And as we grow in our intimacy with Him, we need to allow Him to lead us where He knows we must go, and we must pack what He knows we need for the journey and get rid of the rest. That means that we have to know what baggage we're already dragging around and learn how to become willing to deal with it, as God requires. That process is what is so painful.

Following in bloodstained footprints

We know from Scripture that the twelve men who would become the apostles all came to Jesus with their own preconceptions of what being a Christ-follower would mean, for them and for the world. But after three and a half years of living in a genuine, personal and intimate relationship with their Messiah, these men had been truly transformed and their thinking completely reorientated. History tells us that the personal awakening to the 'who do you say that I am?' in Matthew 16 led each of these apostles down incredibly world-changing paths. From what I can tell from history and from Church tradition, that world-changing hope and faith they'd built their lives on when they chose to align themselves with Jesus and allow Him to become their personal Christ, was one of extreme suffering. It's not pretty reading, but these men are the founding fathers of our faith; this is their story and the story of how the movement of the Christian Church started; it's what happens when men choose to follow and walk with Jesus, their Christ…

It is said that Paul was beheaded, Peter was crucified upside down, Andrew, Philip and Matthias (who replaced Judas) were also crucified, Bartholomew was flayed (which is beyond barbaric!) and then crucified, Thomas was pierced through with spears and then burnt alive, Matthew (the tax collector) was beheaded, James (who was also known as James the Lesser) was stoned and then beaten with clubs, Judas Thaddeus was also beaten with sticks, Simon the Zealot was sawn in two then crucified, and in Acts 12:2 we read that James (John's brother) was executed by the sword. John ended up being the only one of those originally handpicked by Jesus to follow in His footprints, not to die a martyr's death. Although tradition says he went through his own fair share of torture and persecution for the Christian faith, including somehow surviving an attempt to burn him alive in a human-sized pot of boiling oil.

These men discovered that no matter what came their way, they had that hope. And they were so sure of this because of what they had received from *being with Jesus*, that they were prepared to endure anything God would allow to come upon them. They saw it all as a price worthy of paying, because they knew what God had in store for each one of them. We too, who follow in their footsteps, must also find that switch that will turn on that same light for ourselves. I have shared about how the apostles endured to death to stay close to the Christ that they knew intimately, I have talked of the Desert Fathers, who chased Christ into the wilderness and beyond, and I have talked about countless others who knew what it meant to forsake all for the pearl of great price. Anything less than that is not the real Jesus and will forever leave us stumbling over the dry and stale bread of our brokenness. We must, to quote C. Baxter Kruger again, 'Be willing to rethink everything we thought we knew. For it is only as we have our mental instruments revised that we are able to see more clearly, and only as we see more clearly that we experience the liberation and joy and life of such clearer sight.'[17]

Just as those gigantic masses of gas that flood the night sky in the form of stars offer little more than twinklings or flecks to us here on earth, so these pinhole twinklings of hope and faith that we see in our own lives, though they may feel far off, are still huge bushfires of truth that will light up our darkness if we will let them. They are signposts and compass points that remind us that even if the darkness hides the way from us at this moment, 1 Corinthians 10:13 stands true, that God will never let any of us down nor will He ever let us be pushed past our limit; God will always be there to help each of us make it through the night, the storm, the doldrums… we *will* see the sun rise and we *will* see the beauty of a new day.

No matter how painful or how costly, as we wade through the muddied waters of our suffering, we must be determined to make it out onto the other side. The author of the letter to the Hebrews tells us that

> we'd better get on with it. Strip down, start running – and never quit! No extra spiritual fat, no parasitic sins. Keep your eyes on Jesus, who both began and finished this race we're in. Study how he did it. Because he never lost sight of where he was headed – that exhilarating finish in and with God – he could put up with anything along the way: Cross, shame, whatever. And now he's *there*, in the place of honor, right alongside God. When you find yourself flagging in your faith, go over that story again, item by item, that long litany of hostility he plowed through. *That* will shoot adrenaline into your souls![18]

Take Time

Each of the following statements is a quote from this chapter. As we take some time here, read each one and think about how it makes you feel.

- 'I see [pain] as a giver of freedom'
- 'God whispers to us in our pleasures ... but shouts in our pain'
- 'endurance must do its complete work, so that you may be mature and complete, lacking nothing'
- 'don't try to get out of anything prematurely'
- They were prepared to endure anything God would allow to come upon them ... they had that hope
- 'hope is what makes the human condition liveable'

David cried out, 'Investigate my life, O God, find out everything about me; Cross-examine and test me, get a clear picture of what I'm about'.[19] He was willing to lay it all before God. Are you willing to do the same?

Pray

Oh God, Hebrews 12 tells me that when I find myself flagging in my faith, to fix my eyes on Christ, who both began and finished this race I'm in. To study how He did it. You also tell me that You came to help, to put the world right.[20] You tell me that I won't have to stumble around in the darkness because you provide plenty of light.[21]

But God, it is so hard to find freedom in my pain; to endure it; to not try to get out of this process prematurely... I want out, right now!

So please, God, take my hand! Lead me to that place of hope where the apostles lived. Help me not simply endure, but break through the door to where I can look at my life and see that cost of the pearl really is a price worth paying; help me to see what You have in store for me. In faith, not yet seeing, I declare:

GOD – you got me out of that mess,

… I yelled for help
and you put me together.
… You did it: you changed wild lament
into whirling dance;
You ripped off my black mourning band
and decked me with wildflowers.
I'm about to burst with song;
I can't keep quiet about you.
GOD, my God,
I can't thank you enough.[22]

Amen.

Chapter Eight:
Profit of Suffering

Teach me to profit by the suffering that comes across my path.[1]
Cardinal John Henry Newman

We closed out the last chapter with *encouragement* from the writer of Hebrews – 'get on with it … never quit!' Maybe it's the point but those words sound more like those of my high school coach before we ran out against the big, ugly brutes we beat in rugby championship finals; or like that well-worn rallying cry from Britain's great Second World War era Prime Minister, Winston Churchill. I found it tough to hear them as a faith-filled biblical truth, spoken as a hope-hook that I could hang the very future of my life on.

But in saying that, I've always had an issue with Churchill's grand statement too. As the story goes, Churchill was asked to give a speech to the boys of his old high school. When he stood in front of them, he is famously quoted as saying:

Never, ever, ever, ever, ever, ever, ever, give up.
Never give up. Never give up. Never give up.

It's a nice little rev-up, but the quote doesn't offer any sort of hope – to simply slap someone on the back and send them on their way, to *soldier on* is almost a double cruelty. Talk is cheap;

anyone can stand up and tell you to bear your cross, especially when they're not the ones having their backs ripped apart by its splinters.

But to my relief, that's not what Churchill actually said, nor was it how he intended it to be heard by those boys he was addressing. Rather than a glib wartime slogan, he was hinting at something much deeper, almost echoing the words of the writer of the book of Hebrews. When Sir Winston Churchill stood in front of those boys what he actually said was this:

Never, never, in nothing great or small, large or petty, never give in except to convictions of honour and good sense. Never yield to force; never yield to the apparently overwhelming might of the enemy.[2]

He was driving into those young minds the truth that no matter what life has served you or throws at you, no matter how overwhelming the enemy, do not yield to its power. Never quit! But the writer to the Hebrews takes it further. He said this:

Keep your eyes on *Jesus*, who both began and finished this race we're in. Study how he did it. Because he never lost sight of where he was headed ... he could put up with anything along the way: Cross, shame, whatever ... When you find yourselves flagging in your faith, go over that story again, item by item, that long litany of hostility he ploughed through ... others have suffered far worse than you, to say nothing of what Jesus went through—all that bloodshed! So don't feel sorry for yourselves ...

... God is educating you; that's why you must never drop out. He's treating you as dear children ...God is doing what is best

for us, training us to live God's holy best ...
So don't sit around on your hands! No more dragging your
feet ... Help each other out. And run for it ...[3]

If you've ever read the book of Job you'll know that after thirty-
seven chapters of Job and his friends questioning and searching
for the answers about why Satan seemed to have complete and
total freedom to rain down utter agony on Job, God had some
questions of His own. When God spoke, His questions were in
response to rather than in defence of the preceding chapters.
And it was after these questions that the light of God's Spirit
finally turns on for Job and he *gets* it. In reply, Job says to God:

I'm convinced: You can do anything and everything.
Nothing and no one can upset your plans.
You asked, 'Who is this muddying the water,
ignorantly confusing the issue, second-guessing my purposes?'
I admit it. I was the one. I babbled on about things far beyond
me,
made small talk about wonders way over my head.
You told me, 'Listen, and let me do the talking.
Let me ask the questions. You give the answers.'
I admit I once lived by rumors of you;
now I have it all firsthand – from my own eyes and ears!
I'm sorry – forgive me. I'll never do that again, I promise!
I'll never again live on crusts of hearsay, crumbs of rumor.[4]

I must learn from Job

I have always hated reading the book of Job. It was as if there
was some kind of Job disease that I could catch from it. When
Hugh Ross decided to publish a book about lessons we can

learn from Job, he wrote:

> My friends cautioned me not to write this book. They warned
> me, 'No one who attempts to write any kind of commentary on
> Job can escape without some new experience in suffering …
> Almost immediately my friends' cautions proved prophetic.[5]

But God has shown me that I must learn from Job. This man's
life was besieged with enough trauma to kill a man's soul ten
times over and yet at the end of it all, after everything that he
was forced to endure, he makes an utterly definitive statement:
'I'm convinced'. The King James Bible uses the word 'know'. This
knowing or *convinced-ness* (if there is such a word) is a learned
thing. Job didn't wake up one morning and stumble across this
realisation in the same way I wake up and stumble across the
kids' shoes scattered across my living room floor.

For Job to declare that 'Nothing and no one can upset [God's]
plans'… that is a learned truth, it is a faith lesson that God had to
personally teach to His servant. And the heavenly Teacher never
quit, even to the point of tragedy upon tragedy. As a result of
God's loving persistence, Job finally admits that his faith up to
that point had been built on crusts and crumbs, whispers and
rumours.

But 'never again', Job says – 'I'm convinced'!

And now, all these generations and lifetimes later, here we are
once again, standing in the shadows of all those who have gone
before us – others who have also had to wrestle and claw at the
foot of the cross for answers to their own tragedy. And just as
they have done, we stand overwhelmed with our own desolation
and despair. Yet Job's statement still stands as a truth-banner –
after all I have been through, I AM CONVINCED that God was

the author and finisher of my story. I AM CONVINCED that God is the very source of my hope and it is *only* He who can offer me the answers that I seek.

Like Job, even if it means that we'll have to endure to the utmost, we have to find a way to sit through whatever lesson God is trying to teach us, watching Him and learning from him alone, so that we too can declare, 'I AM CONVINCED!'

We must find the way that works for us in our own story, to set aside the second-hand whispers and rumours we thought we could build our hope on because the old way obviously hasn't worked. I just love the way that Eugene Peterson interpreted the words of Hebrews 12: 'Keep your eyes on *Jesus*; Study [Him] … God is educating you; that's why you must never drop out … get on with it'! These are not just rousing words, not some 'punch in the arm' and a 'She'll be right, mate' approach.[6] No, this is a clear call to action from the great I Am. The God of heaven and earth is calling each one of us to choose to become His disciple, or student. No matter how we slice it, if we want to find hope and relief from the burning fires of our past that still smoulder, we must learn of Him *through* our pain. It was the answer for Job, it was the answer for the apostles and early Church disciples, and it is the answer for us.

I had to fight my way through the clutter of my life to find God. I found it far too easy, rather than keep my eyes on Christ, to look at and study my dad, to learn from him. I made the mistake of demanding from him something he could never give – release from my pain. Instead, my hope needed to be in God because He is the only one who promises to take away all my grief, crying and pain. One day my heavenly dad will wipe the tears from my eyes.[7] And that's what makes the words of Job and the book of Hebrews, of Winston Churchill and of my high school coach so important. We are in a battle for our lives, and we need to be roused and pushed forward. We need to be reminded not to quit, to search on; to give it all we've got.

The only way to reach God

My greatest hurdle over the last few years was figuring out how to fumble my way back to that childlike faith I used to have as a kid, when I couldn't take my eyes off Jesus. Back then I knew that the best place to be was with Him, but life had dulled my vision and dented my Christianity. That's why all that fumbling for God was also one of the best things I could ever have done. It was what made me able to cling to the hand of Christ and really see God, as He wants me to see Him. The Bible makes it startlingly clear that until I see past the struggles going on in my head, feel past the aching pain in my heart and fix my eyes on Jesus, I'd never get to the Father. Jesus tells us that, 'no man cometh unto the Father, but by me'; 'No one gets to the Father apart from me'; 'No one comes to the Father except through me'.[8] The only way to reach God, so that we can discover for ourselves the truths that Job became convinced of, is through truly getting to know Jesus Christ.

But He also says, 'If you make yourselves at home with me and my words are at home in you, you can be sure that whatever you ask will be listened to and acted upon ... I've told you these things for a purpose: that my joy might be your joy, and your joy wholly mature.'[9]

And I get the feeling that Jesus spoke these words because He knew me. He knew that we humans falter when the road we are walking looks bleak and endless. So this Man of Sorrows, acquainted with grief,[10] reaches out a holy hand of comfort. The psalmist is far more urgent in the way he expresses the point in

Psalm 27: 'Stay with GOD! Take heart. Don't quit. I'll say it again: Stay with GOD.'[11]

Looking back through this experience of examining my life, my pain and the way ahead, I realise that all I ever really wanted to do was to stay *with* God. I don't want to quit. Instead, I want to tap into what God has for me, and I want that to be like an IV line pumping me full of the joy and life of Christ. That will only happen when I leave room for God to do what He needs to do, because growth comes when we let go and allow God to act.

As a man once wrote:

I've tried everything and nothing helps. I'm at the end of my rope. Is there no one who can do anything for me? Isn't that the real question? The answer, thank God, is that Jesus Christ can and does. He acted to set things right in this life of contradictions where I want to serve God with all my heart and mind …

… God went for the jugular when he sent his own Son. He didn't deal with the problem as something remote and unimportant. In his Son, Jesus, he personally took on the human condition and entered the disordered mess of struggling humanity in order to set it right once and for all …

It stands to reason, doesn't it, that if the alive-and-present God who raised Jesus from the dead moves into your life, he'll do the same thing in you that he did in Jesus, bringing you alive to himself? When God lives and breathes in you (and he does, as surely as he did in Jesus), you are delivered from that dead life.

… God's Spirit beckons. There are things to do and places to go! This resurrection life you received from God is not a timid, grave-tending life. It's adventurously expectant, greeting God with a childlike 'What's next, Papa?' God's Spirit touches our spirits and confirms who we really are. We know who he is, and we know who we are: Father and children. And we know we are going to get what's coming to us – an unbelievable inheritance!

... the moment we get tired in the waiting, God's Spirit is right alongside helping us along. If we don't know how or what to pray, it doesn't matter. He does our praying in and for us, making prayer out of our wordless sighs, our aching groans. He knows us far better than we know ourselves ... That's why we can be so sure that every detail in our lives of love for God is worked into something good ...

So, what do you think? With God on our side like this, how can we lose? If God didn't hesitate to put everything on the line for us, embracing our condition and exposing himself to the worst by sending his own Son, is there anything else he wouldn't gladly and freely do for us? And who would dare tangle with God by messing with one of God's chosen? Who would dare even to point a finger? The One who died for us—who was raised to life for us!—is in the presence of God at this very moment sticking up for us. Do you think anyone is going to be able to drive a wedge between us and Christ's love for us? There is no way! Not trouble, not hard times, not hatred, not hunger, not homelessness, not bullying threats, not backstabbing, not even the worst sins listed in Scripture ...

... None of this fazes us because Jesus loves us. I'm absolutely convinced that nothing – nothing living or dead, angelic or demonic, today or tomorrow, high or low, thinkable or unthinkable – absolutely *nothing* can get between us and God's love because of the way that Jesus our Master has embraced us.[12]

Those words, penned by a guy once named Saul of Tarsus, have stood the test of time. More than 2,000 years after they were scratched onto a piece of dried parchment, they are still vibrant and true. After he had gone through the Hall of Faith, the writer to the Hebrews reminds us that 'Not one of these people, even though their lives of faith were exemplary, got their hands on what was promised. God had a better plan …'[13]

God has a plan for each of us too, so

don't shrug off God's discipline,
but don't be crushed by it either.
It's the child he loves that he disciplines;
the child he embraces, he also corrects.
God is educating you; that's why you must never drop out.
He's treating you as dear children. This trouble you're in isn't punishment; it's training … do you see how thankful we must be? Not only thankful, but brimming with worship, deeply reverent before God. For God is not an indifferent bystander. He's actively cleaning house, torching all that needs to burn, and he won't quit until it's all cleansed. God himself is Fire![14]

Take Time

In a moment, I am going to ask you to pray a very simple prayer with me. It's the prayer from Cardinal John Henry Newman that headed this chapter:

Teach me to profit by the suffering that comes across my path.[15]

But first, as we take some time here, I encourage you to ask God for an open mind and heart for what He is revealing to you.

- The Bible reminds us that God has a better plan for each of us and that He will work every detail of our lives into something good. It also reminds us, in the verses from Hebrews we closed the chapter with, that the troubles we face are, in fact, not trouble at all. God speaks here, letting you know that what you have been through in your life is God-ordained fire to bring you to the place of wholeness; more than that – the burning in your life is God Himself and He is training you.

  This is not an easy concept, especially for those of us who have experienced the burning fire of very real human pain. Yet Hebrews says that you should not only be thankful for it, but brimming with worship because God is at work in your life with it. You might not be able to comprehend how that lines up to the God of love that you have been raised to know, and that's OK. If you need to, ask the Holy Spirit, the Breath of God, to breathe peace, clarity and grace into your heart and soul as you do business with God over it. And do business with God – wrestle with the Scriptures and the perceived injustice and unfairness of it all. It's what I did!

- When you feel ready to move on, read through Hebrews 12 again and pray that God would help you hear His voice speaking directly to you.

- Are you ready to join me in prayer?

Pray

Dear heavenly Father,
Teach me to profit by the suffering that comes across my path. Help me see it as holy fire lit not by an indifferent bystander, but set alight by a loving Father who is using it for my good.
Amen.

Chapter Nine:
My Idea of God

My idea of God is not a divine idea. It has to be shattered time after time. He shatters it Himself.[1]
C.S. Lewis

One of the greatest secrets to success is being able to admit when something isn't working and having the ability to find and move into a way that does. And it's that particular thought process that makes this next step perhaps one of the most pivotal to our Christian walk. Jesus told His Father, 'not My will, but Yours, be done'.[2] And we are called to do the same. That means that we have to take all we have known and all that we have believed in and we have to lay it all down at the feet of our Lord.

The reason we need to do this is because something ain't quite right – if the way we have been walking as Christians, or as the Church, was, in fact, the *right way* for us to somehow solve the issues of pain and forgiveness in our individual lives, I have no doubt we would have streams of people lined up outside churches wanting what we've got. I don't see that queue because there are too many wounded, disillusioned Christians in the world. I have lived my life hoping that one day I would wake up in the morning no longer in the valley. My thinking was that, while I might have a limp, I was supposed to be living on the mountaintop. I was certain that if I trusted in God, my past would somehow be rubbed out and my new day would be full of good. The idea of God writing a messy future was outside my theology of living.

But as my buddy, Kent Evens told me, understanding God and His actions in this world is like trying to understand an architect's design for a building straight after an earthquake has shaken it to smithereens… it makes no sense. And that's why we must acknowledge that life without pain is actually a very dangerous fantasy; a fantasy that is closer to the kind of thinking found in books such as Dale Carnegie's *How to Win Friends and Influence People* than the theology of the Bible. You could spend your whole life searching for answers, and all you'll achieve is this – you'll miss the incredible life that God designed specifically for you. And then, when you do reach the end and you draw your last breath, you'd still be left with the pain you'd spent your life fleeing from. Remember, the whole point of Christ's life here on earth was to take up His cross, and He reminds us to do the same. Just as in Kent's earthquake analogy, the followers of Jesus were left decimated in the aftermath of His crucifixion. It just made no sense.

It was as that thought sunk in, I realised my need to take the time to meditate on God's plan for me, rather than to focus my expectations on my vision or version of God's plan for my life. I love how Paulo Coelho talked about this in his sweet little allegorical novel, *The Alchemist*. He wrote that, 'We are afraid of losing what we have, whether it's our life or our possessions and property. But this fear evaporates when we understand that our life stories and the history of the world were written by the same hand.'[3]

My life, all of it, has been written by God's hand. In fact, 'the life of every living thing is in His hand, as well as the breath of all mankind'.[4] And when God's Spirit opened my eyes and enabled me to come to grips with that concept, in all its complexity and fullness, it allowed me to look again at my understanding of God and the expectations of how He was supposed to act. With grace and wisdom, God freed my heart from the chains that were dragging me down into misery. He allowed me to see that I didn't need to attribute blame or fault; I didn't need to see regret or remorse from those who had caused me pain. How they chose to live their lives was their choice. But my life was and is His gift to me, and how I choose to live it was, and always will always be, my gift to Him.

Freedom is an incredible thing – it has enabled me to choose to let go of injustice and my need for restitution. God has told me that because He holds me in His palm and my life is written by His hand, it doesn't matter what comes:

I, your GOD,
have a firm grip on you and I'm not letting go.
I'm telling you, 'Don't panic.
I'm right here to help you.[5]

Here is the plain truth

God loves me. The complexities come when I try to interpret the language of heaven through the lens of my experience. I think this idea is a stumbling block for most of us. Somewhere along the walk of faith we have bought into the idea that God would or should act in exactly the same way that we would act, if it were us standing in His shoes. And that's why, as C.S. Lewis wrote, He has to shatter my idea of God, because it's not a divine idea – we humans have a great way of creating our own ideas about who God is. The problem with carving out our own image of God is that He's governed and limited by our own humanity; He can only do what we are capable of allowing Him to do. Even worse is that our eyes no longer search out the genuine reality and presence of the God who *is*.

No matter how life appears, what has happened or what will happen, 'GOD is striding ahead of you. He's right there with you. He won't let you down; he won't leave you. Don't be intimidated. Don't worry.'[6] Jesus dying on the cross proves it – God has not forsaken any of His children. Jesus hangs up there for all of humanity to see, from BC to AD, that God loves each one of us with an immoveable, unstoppable love… God sent His Son into the highways and byways and told Him to spend it all to bring us home. And that's exactly what Jesus did!

If God is at work in every detail of our lives, if Jesus Christ is the source of our hope, how do we push past church culture and tradition to access it? I've spent a lot of my life travelling the world, meeting lots of different types of people, and experiencing some very different and unusual cultures. One thing that struck me about the way in which I react to or absorb all those experiences and people is just how much my own upbringing, my own beliefs and values, have formed my views. So much of what I like, or don't like – food, politics, whatever – has been shaped by where I was born, the family I was born into, the life choices I've made. And it is the same with my view of God, of Jesus. My whole perception of who I am as a Christian has been moulded and guided by other men's hands and other men's traditions… I have just never fully realised it.

And, for the record, this is no new discovery – it is an issue that has troubled men and women for centuries. In 1797, the now-famous abolitionist, William Wilberforce, penned these words:

I hope you don't think I am being arrogant or overly harsh on cultural Christians. Look at the facts. Do cultural Christians view Christian faith as important enough to make a priority when teaching their children what they believe and why they believe it? Or do they place greater emphasis on their children getting a good education than on learning about the things of God? ... If the children view themselves as Christians, it is probably not because they have studied the facts and come to a point of intellectual conviction but because their family is Christian, so they believe they must be Christian also. The problem with this way of thinking is that authentic faith cannot be inherited. When Christianity is viewed in this way, intelligent and energetic young men and women will undoubtedly reach a point where they question the truth of Christianity and, when challenged, will abandon this 'inherited' faith that they cannot defend. They might begin to associate with peers who are unbelievers. In this company, they will find themselves unable to respond to objections to Christianity with which they are confronted. Had they really known what they believe and why they believe it, these kinds of encounters would not shake their faith one bit. I fear for the future of authentic faith in our country...[7]

Is God doing wrong?

God wants us to know Him for ourselves because a passed-on experience or inherited relationship is no way to build a true friendship. True friendship leads to an all-embracing intimacy and trust; completely letting go of the wheel, knowing that God is a better driver than you anyway. But even the great men of faith struggled over how to figure that out. Job was 'honest inside and out, a man of his word, who was totally devoted to God and hated evil with a passion'.[8] Yet he struggled over this for thirty-seven chapters and in the end, God really put him in his place:

> Now what do you have to say for yourself?
> Are you going to haul me, the Mighty One, into court and
> press charges?
> … Do you presume to tell me what I'm doing wrong?
> Are you calling me a sinner so you can be a saint?
> Do you have an arm like my arm?
> Can you shout in thunder the way I can?
> Go ahead, show your stuff.
> Let's see what you're made of, what you can do.
> Unleash your outrage.
> … I'll gladly step aside and hand things over to you –
> you can surely save yourself with no help from me![9]

God said those same words to me as He was dealing with my
junk too. He took me to the book of Isaiah:

> Woe to the one who argues with his Maker –
> one clay pot among many.
> Does clay say to the one forming it,
> 'What are you making?'
> Or does your work say,
> 'He has no hands'?
> How absurd is the one who says to his father,
> 'What are you fathering?'
> or to his mother,
> 'What are you giving birth to?'[10]

And then in the letter to the Ephesians:
> God has us where he wants us, with all the time in this world

and the next to shower grace and kindness upon us in Christ Jesus. Saving is all his idea, and all his work. All we do is trust him enough to let him do it. It's God's gift from start to finish! We don't play the major role. If we did, we'd probably go around bragging that we'd done the whole thing! No, we neither make nor save ourselves. God does both the making and saving. He creates each of us by Christ Jesus to join him in the work he does, the good work he has gotten ready for us to do, work we had better be doing.[11]

And He showed me how this was playing out in my life and through the lives of so many others throughout the Bible and the rest of history. While God showed me that for as long as I live and breathe I will experience difficulties and suffering, He also promised to hand me the compass, to lead me, to look after me and protect me when I fall. Listen to what God says to us through Jeremiah the prophet: 'When you come looking for me, you'll find me.'[12] Solomon tells us that those who look for God will find him. Moses explains in the books of the law that 'if you seek GOD, your God, you'll be able to find him if you're serious, looking for him with your whole heart and soul.'[13] He also tells us that 'When troubles come and all these awful things happen to you ... he will not abandon you, he won't bring you to ruin.'[14] And if you are left in any doubt at all:

Here's what I'm saying:
Ask and you'll get;
Seek and you'll find;
Knock and the door will open.
Don't bargain with God. Be direct. Ask for what you need.
This is not a cat-and-mouse, hide-and-seek game we're in.[15]

Over and over again, God tells us that when we look for Him, we'll find Him: '... Yes, when you get serious about finding me and want it more than anything else, I'll make sure you won't be disappointed.'[16]

This is Scripture and that means you can hold on to it! I know because I've had to. I have seen first-hand that when God promises to guide us, He will do it – He will lead us to the very place we need to go. But He wants us to learn this for ourselves, and that's the reason His hand so often directs us through the valley of the shadow of death – so that we do get serious about finding Him, and want that more than anything else.

'Do you see what I've done?' God says, 'I've refined you, but not without fire. I've tested you like silver in the furnace of affliction.'[17] It is here, in the crucible, that we'll discover more of His nature and character; it is here we learn how to reach out to Him and to call on Him; it is here we fall in love with our Saviour because we experience a deeper portion of His love. 'Yes, Onward, Christian! the captain of your salvation hath gone through the dark valley before you – therefore, onward! Onward with boldness! Onward with courage! Onward with hope! that ye may be like your Saviour, by participation in his sufferings.'[18]

Take Time

We opened this chapter with a quote from C.S. Lewis' book, *A Grief Observed*. The book was never written to be published, but was taken from the journals he wrote after the death of his wife. The pages are filled with such raw anguish and, as its introduction says, 'is a stark recounting of one man's studied attempts to come to grips with and in the end defeat the emotional paralysis of the most shattering grief of his life.'[19]

This is the background to his words, 'My idea of God is not a divine idea. It has to be shattered time after time. He shatters it Himself.'[20] And it's also his licence to speak into our pain right now as we take some time to consider what we've just read. You don't have to agree with all of this here and now, but take as much time as you need and be as honest as you can. And as you do, I want to pray for you.

God, I thank you so much that You promise us that the life of every living thing is in Your hand and You have each of us right where You want us.

I am so grateful that You have a firm grip on each one of us; that we can be sure that You are not letting go.

You tell us not to panic, but as You shatter our constructs of You and of our Christian faith that are built with our own hands, I beg that You shower Your grace and kindness upon us and fill us with Your perfect love, for perfect love casts out all fear, as we read in 1 John 4:18.

We are knocking, God; we are serious about finding You. We want it more than anything else!

You, Lord, have gone through the dark valley before us. I pray for courage and for hope for the ones You love, God, for the ones reading this book right now.

Help them to see that You haven't abandoned them, nor will You bring them to ruin. Instead, as they let go and lay down their expectations and hopes, help them to gladly step aside and hand things over to You.

Amen.

And now, here are some questions for you. Pray through each one and be kind to yourself. Remember you can take your time with them; you can even note down that you don't know where to park the thought, or that it's maybe just too challenging. At the end, there's a short prayer too.

- What is your idea of God? Would you agree with Lewis that perhaps it's more your own construct? And if that is the case, are you willing to lay that down right now?
- Are you willing to acknowledge that God is the captain of the ship of your past, present and future? Can you say that He is the architect of your life?
- Are you able to confess that your life, all of it, has been written by God's hand?

Pray
I am the clay,
You are the Potter,
Mould me, God!
Amen.

Part Three:
The Road to Healing

Chapter Ten:
Make a New Ending

You cannot go back and make a new start, but you can start now and make a new ending.[1]
The Almond Tree (a novel)

There's no escaping the fact that my past is what it is – that part of my existence that has already happened. It shaped me and has probably affected every area of my life. Tragically, it's that past that so often leaves us like Joseph,[2] at the bottom of a pit – alone, confused, and thinking there is no way out. But nothing could be further from the truth to God. He has a purpose and a plan; nothing is wasted. God is determined to use the well-worn road that now lies behind each one of us, as the starting point of our future. As Pascal wrote almost four centuries ago: 'People are generally better persuaded by the reasons which they have themselves discovered than by those which have come into the mind of others.'[3]

Through the act of Christ's sacrifice on the cross, God reaches down from heaven into our individual stories to help us move forward. At this very moment I am completely free to choose what my tomorrow will look like… I can slump back down into the crater of despondency or I can grab the rope of a hope and future that Jesus handed me, and climb.

Yes, the road that leads to life is tough and narrow. And sure, I may slip and stumble a few times. But that's why it is written:

> "No eye has seen, no ear has heard, and no mind has imagined what God has prepared for those who love him."[4]

What an adventure stands before us! So onward, Christian – search out the best path forward, commit to it and press on with boldness, courage and hope!

It's here that I have to press the 'pause' button and call a time-out. It's one thing to get all fired-up and excited, but when I got to this point in my journey I felt like David Livingstone, the famous missionary and explorer of Africa as he stood on the edge of the great African unknown. I found myself needing some answers:

- What does this *Great adventure* with God look like in my Christian walk?
- Where do I go from here?
- What are the signposts that I can use to navigate the way?
- What is the best way forward?
- What do I do with what I've learned so far, for it to become a powerful tool in my life?
- How do I turn it into a roadmap that leads me to the treasure of healing, forgiveness and hope?

This is the point where each one of us must ask for God's help; to be the lamp to *our* feet and that light to *our* path, as David says in Psalm 119. He promises that we don't have to stumble forward in the darkness… Jesus told us in John 14 that His Holy Spirit, whom He left with us, will make everything plain and easy to understand. God's Spirit constantly reminds us of all the things God has taught us. Jesus also says in John 14 that we won't feel abandoned or deserted, upset or distraught, because His Holy Spirit is with us. He is from God and of God, our source and Creator; if He made us, He knows how to fix us, how to unknot our lives. I am learning to trust that He knows the way, no matter how unknown it might be to me.

I've found that this is such a personal part of our process or walk. It's the *closet* stuff, where each one of us needs to hide ourselves away in prayer with God. I need to seek His way for *me* and you need to seek your way. Individually, each one of us must sit with God and unfold the map that He drew up for the road *we* must travel. I don't mean that we create our own version of God or a personalised version of the Christian faith – there is only one way to the Father, and that is through the Son. What I'm saying is that now is the time for each of us to truly open our hearts to the light and love of God. We must choose to allow His strength to flow through every part of us, to reach each pain and every hurt. Job had to learn for himself and to know for himself that God is real, before God allowed Satan to take his foot from Job's throat – and so do we.

I'll share my experience of learning for myself in the next chapter. But right now as we launch, or possibly lurch, forward in this great adventure of faith, running into what might be completely scary and unknown to us, let's start with a question.

What does it mean to be a Christian?

If you were to really ask yourself that question, I suggest that it would look something like the life you are currently living, just on a higher, slightly out-of-reach level; a holiness you earnestly desire but perhaps feel like you can never quite fully attain. Does that sound about right?

I think that most Christians believe that if they simply

continue to walk 'in the right direction', on the road they are on right now, they'll become more and more like Jesus. And that may well be true, but what if it's not? What if God has a much lower expectation of you? Even writing that statement causes me to take a breath... I'm still trying to really understand the full ramifications of such a possibility.

But let's unpack that some more. I'm not suggesting that God doesn't call us to live *better, higher, holier*. But that wasn't my question. The question is, 'What does it mean to be a Christian?' For the longest time, I think I missed the point of who I became when I was saved, and what it means in terms of healing from a past life of chaos. And I'm not alone. I have spoken to so many Christians who all come up with a different version of how we are supposed to live once we have crossed this bridge into faith.

From what I understand, the followers of Jesus became known as 'Christians' because they believed Jesus of Nazareth was the Messiah (or *Christos*), prophesied in the Hebrew Bible. Today, we are asked that very same question: 'Do you believe that Jesus is the Christ?'

If you are anything like me, you'll be stumbling over that last paragraph with something like, 'Well, of course I do, but...' because our humanness tells us that while that's true, there are other things we need to do to maintain our faith or be better disciples.

Could it be that simple? Could it be really be possible that God isn't actually standing in front of us with a test sheet? Instead, He's just waiting for the words, 'I believe You are the Christ.' If the answer to that is 'yes' then I would imagine it'd be a good idea to pause and to contemplate what that means. To me, I read it as saying that it's OK to stop trying to figure out what it means to be a Christian; it's OK to stop trying to live a certain way. It is actually OK to stop *trying* to please God. It's OK because the answer to forgiveness and to healing and hope is not found in trying to do any of those things.

Instead, we need to take some time (say, the rest of our life) to get to know the Christ; the One who didn't come and die *just* to save us from our sins or save us *for* heaven. As mind-blowing as that is, this Jesus of Nazareth did something else that was as equally profound – through the cross of Calvary, Jesus let me see God and gave me the ability to get to know Him personally.

God wants *me* to know Him!

Those six words take up such a small amount of space on the page, but behind them is an absolute and profound truth. When Jesus hung up on that rough piece of timber, he yelled out into the afternoon sky, 'I've paid the price, its done!'[5] or words to that effect. The job was done; the curtain pulled back. We could now peek into heaven where God sits, we could see God and we could *know* Him. Don't miss this, because it's kind of a big deal. Moses didn't even get that, nor did Abraham or David or Solomon, Daniel, Isaiah, Jeremiah or any of the other big-name Bible guys. But God saw fit that you and I get to... right now we can glimpse the face of God. And get this – we get to see that face full of love and mercy and compassion not just glancing back at us but earnestly seeking us.

The God of the universe is looking for you.

I have read and reread that statement to try to find a way to convey just how awesome and unfathomable the reality of that fact is to me. I have looked at it; I've pondered it; I read what it means in the original language; I have searched what the writers of the Gospels were really trying to tell us about what it means to *know* someone. But no matter how I try to get my head around the mind-bending reality of what God did and is continuing to do through Jesus Christ, so that I could know him... Nope, I still think I'm missing getting the impact across.

Hold on to that thought and I'll try to get there from another angle. When Jesus was wandering the dusty roads of northern Israel a couple of thousand years ago, He was asked about the greatest or most important thing we should be doing with our limited time here on earth. He tells us that the greatest thing we can do is...

'Love God.'

'... Oh, and by the way, it's just as important to love others as you love yourself.'

Essentially Jesus tells us that if you were to sum up all the Old and New Testament writings, they all boil down to that one phrase – love God, and love others as much as yourself.

I have to put my hand up here and tell you I have been guilty of not doing this. I didn't set my heart and mind to this most important task Jesus spoke of. Instead, I set up more of what the Israelites set up – some form of structure and rulebook by which to live my life. I set up a bunch of fences to make sure that I didn't inadvertently stumble out of His favour and into some place that'd make God unhappy with me. I mean, who wants to be a sinner in the hands of an angry God, right? And then when things didn't go quite right, I figured that all of my pain and all of my weaknesses were a spiritual reminder that I wasn't good enough for God. I'd try harder to act better, think better, break less of the 'God rules' that I had deemed were the most important to my Christian walk. We've probably all done this at least once in our lives. What God is showing me as I go through the healing process of writing this book is that so much of what we believe, or think we believe, is built off the backs of others. And some of what we think we believe to be spiritual truths may have nothing whatsoever to do with God's heart on the matter.

With the pure faith and excitement that could move mountains, I intentionally asked Jesus to be *my* Jesus when I was four. But from that point I went on to build my own picture of who this Jesus I was worshipping actually was. As you'd expect, to do that I looked at what my parents believed and drew so many of my faith principles from them. But as a result, when I read the Bible, it spoke in the same way my mum and dad spoke. The foundations of my faith were, in reality, planks from my parents and from their worldview. Don't get me wrong, grasping your faith from your parents is a very biblical approach, but the point I'm making here is that we need to acknowledge that a lot of what we believe (or think we believe) is actually not our own. The reality is that an awful lot of our Christianity is borrowed, absorbed and acquired.

As I grew in my faith I went to hear speakers my parents took me to, read their books and learned to build a spiritual life much like theirs. My dad seemed, to my young eyes, to have the eyes of God Himself. He could see what God saw and He would speak words that shook hearers because of their prophetic accuracy. And my mum had the most incredibly unshakeable faith. Despite everything that seemed to be thrown her way, she would always declare that we will rise up on wings like eagles. No matter how disastrous life was, she passed on to me an unflinching faith that her God would never ever fail her, or me.

I never knew it then, but as I searched more and more to live within the confines of my own ever-solidifying worldview, I started losing something. While trying to be a Christian, and while trying to work out what that really means, I also started to, little bit by little bit, walk away from that young boy who really loved and knew God. I walked further and further towards a deeper Christian walk, trying to find ways to beat the spiritual battles, to live with less sin, to grow in a deeper maturity of faith, to be a better Christian.

But what I see now is that I was in a really unhealthy cycle. I would go through all of this only to discover that I was missing something vital. So I'd try again, always wanting to go deeper in my Christian faith. But that wasn't what Jesus asked of us when He said that our greatest purpose in life is to love God and love others as we love ourselves. If He had wanted us to spend our lives jumping through hoops, Jesus would have said that the greatest commandment is to do all you can to live a life that reflects the perfect nature of God. He would have given us an exhaustive list of *how-tos*. While most of that list would probably be filled with pretty good principles to live our lives by, Jesus didn't seem to think they were important enough to mention. Instead, He said:

Tim, would you spend your whole life getting to know Me and learning to love Me? Would you learn what it means to love Me with your mind, to love Me with your heart, to love Me (a being you can't see, touch or feel) with your body and with your soul? Do you think you could do that?

Oh, and Tim, I want you to learn to love yourself too. When you can do that, love others the same way. I died so that you would see that there is more to Me than a daily prayer or an offering of some kind... come inside the curtain and search for Me.

That line that has made it into every *Terminator* movie, 'come with me if you want to live' was stolen from Christ. He calls us to take our eyes off the dung that life throws at us and grab His hand. It is why I believe that He allows our lives to be so rocky and hard. It has forced me to look to Him, to need Him, and to cry out for Him to fill me with His strength. I can't grab God's hand if I do not love and trust Him; I can't really love Him if I don't know what it means to love or be loved. It's like a trinity of love – the love of God, the love of self and the love of others. If I can't love me, I can't really love God. And what I do to others, I do to God… So I need to learn to love them.

Take Time

- What does it mean to you to be a Christian? As we take some time now to think and pray through that question, maybe write down what you have set up as pillars of your faith. How do they compare with Jesus' *Love God; love others; love yourself* statement we find in the books of Matthew (22:35–40), Mark (12:28–31) and Luke (10:25–28)?

One of the scribes approached. When he heard them debating and saw that Jesus answered them well, he asked Him, "Which command is the most important of all?"

"This is the most important," Jesus answered: Listen, Israel! The Lord our God, the Lord is One. Love the Lord your God with all your heart, with all your soul, with all your mind, and with all your strength.

"The second is: Love your neighbor as yourself.

There is no other command greater than these."[6]

- How do you feel when you think about the simplicity of Christ's words here? Do they bring a sense of fear or of freedom?

I found that teaching so huge that I actually didn't know how or where to start. Did I have to love me before I could love God or other people? Or did I have to love others first? When I sat down with my spiritual advisor with my questions, he asked, 'Which is the hardest for you to do, Tim?'

And I ask you the same question now:

- How do you feel about making a commitment to searching out what it really means to love God? And what about forgiving and loving yourself or doing the same to others?

For me, by the way, I find the hardest thing to do is to love myself. And that has been my starting point. But I have found that all three are actually linked. As you learn to love yourself, you have to deal with those people in your life who have somehow said you aren't worthy of love. You also have to deal with loving a God who allows, causes, pain.

- Do you think you could ask God right now to help you through the process of forgiveness and love? It's not an instant process and you might need to get professional or spiritual help along the way. I needed both. But right now, all I'm asking is that you are willing.

Pray

God, I love You. You've said that no one's ever seen or heard nor even imagined what you have planned for those who love You. If that's true, God, and I believe it is, then help me right now to go anywhere, provided it brings me to a place of love for You and of You. Help me do whatever it takes to learn to love myself and love those who have come through my life. God, You know the pain and heartache behind some of those faces, so be gracious with me during the process. But I want my life to be an instrument of praise, worship and love, so take the wheel. Show me, where do I go from here? God, I give You my life to this point and pray that You would use it as part of Your roadmap for my future. Use it to lead me to Your treasure of healing, forgiveness and hope.

Amen.

Chapter Eleven:
Forgiveness is Power

The only way to diminish the suffering that
burdens mankind is by forgiveness.[1]
Jacques Philippe

I didn't come to be writing a book on forgiveness and healing because I'm some great expert on either of the subjects. I just happened to be a guy willing to explore my own personal journey and the bruises that come with it… while being followed around the world by a camera crew. I was asked to work with Focus on the Family to make a documentary and a series of teachings on the issues facing families today.[2] When I started out working through the making of the project, I presumed it'd be easy because I had my life pretty much figured out. I had a great family – an incredible wife, whom I had met and married young, and my best friend; five beautiful kids, who we'd raised in the right ways; I had a great job as the head of the New Zealand office of Focus on the Family… I was the perfect guy for this job, because I knew what a good, godly example of marriage and family looked like – mine!

But as I was searching, through the making of Focus on the Family's *The Family Project*, for the answers to help everyone else, my life intersected with the lives and thoughts of some of the world's leading experts on the issue of culture and faith, as well as with those who had battled through the realities of it themselves. These interactions were like little chisels and picks, chipping away at the veneer of Tim Sisarich, and helping me see that I wasn't quite as together as I thought I was. I didn't even realise that behind my carefully crafted façade I was desperately trying to find ways to hide my own pain, scrambling to ensure that my marriage and family didn't go the same way as that of my parents'. It became an intimate pilgrimage of personal discovery, where I found myself peeling back old whitewashed mortar I had used to hide my own complicated situation.

In Greece, where we were filming some bits for the introduction to the film series, I met with an Orthodox priest and was blabbering away about my idealist worldview where marriage and family was concerned. I was trying to get my head around what I saw as the huge gulf between my idea of God's best for family and culture versus the things I saw as wrong out there in the real world. This wrinkled old man of the cloth looked at me with his wise eyes, smiled, and said, 'Tim, that's the problem with those of you from the West – you are always trying to fit everyone and everything into your own predetermined box. That is the real danger of a worldview…it is simply your limited view of the world. It is not until any of us have taken the time to listen and learn from others, to hear the different thoughts and views on a matter, that we can say that we've formed a view on anything.' And then he went back to his lunch.

That handful of words was all he spoke to me and they were like water that cracked a tiny seed of hope in my life. It was the genesis of my pilgrimage into *the great embrace* of the One who loves me so much – in His gentle and tender way, God started using people everywhere to reveal a little more of the truth He had been wanting to reveal to me for years. I started to get the hint that my frantic desire to protect my family actually grew out of my own sense of lack; a lack that was birthed out of deep resentment towards my dad. I resented him for not being involved enough as a father, for not keeping me safe from the pitfalls of the culture. I would learn that it actually went much deeper – even though my Christian mantra wouldn't let me admit it (because it was so unchristian), in my heart I hated my dad for what he did to my mum and to his children. This deep-seated wound had blinded me to the real cause of fear and mistrust in my life.

Face-to-face with God

Earlier in this book, I talked about visiting Rembrandt's painting 'The Return of the Prodigal Son' at the Hermitage Museum in St Petersburg, Russia. I had the incredible privilege of being in the museum alone, early one spring morning, as the sun was just starting to peek through the windows of that stunning museum. It was one of those moments you never forget – me, the little film crew I'd been working so closely with for the past several months, and Rembrandt's 350-year old painting.[3] And it was at this unique moment in time that God chose to bring everything I had been gathering together to come smashing into a head-on collision with my carefully constructed Christian life. It didn't matter that I was standing in one of the world's greatest buildings or that I was looking at a canvas painted by one of the world's greatest artists; and it definitely didn't matter that this whole thing was being caught on film – everything peeled away and I found myself alone, face-to-face with God.

First He whispered into my heart, 'Tim, I love you, I love you as you are right at this minute. I'm not waiting for you to *become* the child I love, *you are* the child I love… until you realise that you are My dearly loved prodigal, you will never be able to let go of the pain caused by others.' The instantaneous change to my very core was nothing short of miraculous – my heart softened and my pain and anger towards my dad melted. As the tears streamed down my face, I sensed that God was changing me from being the prodigal of Rembrandt's painting and instead giving me the heart of the father.

God met me there in front of that painting and He made sure I had no doubt that He and I had done business. But then He chose to use my cherished 'God moment' to challenge me to let it all go – all the anger, the justification for the anger, my frustration, my pain… all of it. As He embraced me, God said, 'There is no doubt that My love has changed you, Tim. In the very same way that I have just expressed love for you, love your dad. Love. *Show* him that he is loved. You are not to show him love despite who he is or what he's done, but because you are now the hands of God to that man. Cup his face and help him to see that I love him in all his brokenness, just like I love you in yours.'

It was as if someone had yanked up the handbrake; everything came slamming in around me as I started to comprehend that God was asking me to navigate my way around one of the biggest obstacles that had dogged me my entire life. I always loved God and I trusted Him; when I grew up, He and I were best buddies and I had no doubt that He was truly real. But as I staggered to find my feet that day, I felt like He'd set me up and tricked me into checkmate. There was no way, in my mind, that this was the way my epiphany was supposed to wrap up.

What did I expect?

When I was eleven, I won a school speech competition with a speech called, 'My Best Friend' and it was all about my best friend, Jesus. When I was sixteen, I told God that I didn't want to live with the masks that I had developed to get me through high school. I wanted people to see and know the kid God had made me to be. And when I was nineteen, after being water baptised with Jesmae, the cute wee girl who had, for reasons still unknown to me, agreed to marry me only a couple of months earlier, I declared, 'Wherever, whenever, whatever you call us to do, God, we will do it.'

And I chased that declaration without thought or doubt. I heard God speak with a clarity that I never dreamed to question – I knew His voice, I knew He knew me and I lived with a certainty that *wherever, whenever, whatever*, He would always look after me. But I now see that there was one thing that always hounded me – despite all I claimed to be true and all I claimed to think or believe, I always had an unvoiced and unacknowledged anger and resentment towards my father. That poison become embedded into the bedrock of my entire existence. It left me feeling fractured and disorientated as a boy and then later, insecure and vulnerable as a man. In every part of my life, from my family and job choices to the friends I chose to surround myself with and the church I attended, I became obsessed with finding a *safe* community.

Little did I know then, but my distorted view of the world meant that I felt everyone but God was ultimately going to hurt me and fail me. It was an ongoing fight to feel emotionally or spiritually safe in this world I had constructed, and that's why it was so life-shattering for me when God intentionally pressed on that weakness as He unhinged me that day at the Hermitage.

But God...

There's no doubt in my mind that something changed in me that day that has allowed me to see and hear from God in a very different way. As David wrote, 'GOD rewrote the text of my life when I opened the book of my heart to his eyes.'[4] He has been able to show me over and over again that the suffering that darkens the windows of my soul is part of His process and that it is only ever but a moment to Him. It is the river He uses to carry me closer to His adoring embrace. As I rush downstream into His waiting arms, life's whirlpools and rapids push me on, ensuring I don't climb out onto the bank and settle in the weeds. The tumbling and struggling creates desperation for God, without which I doubt I'd ever really be able to trust in Him enough to let go of all the life that has happened to make Tim Sisarich the person he is. I see that God's act of love so often comes through pain.

God's bumping and prodding may very well be very different for each one of us. For Job, the revelation came only after he lost everything precious to him and God allowing Satan to drag him right to the edge of his life. Only then did Job come to the realisation that God alone could be God. Nothing but discovery could have brought Job to the place where he could say, 'The LORD gave and the LORD has taken away; may the name of the LORD be praised."[5]

For Aleksandr Solzhenitsyn, it came after the utterly unjust sentence of eight years in a Siberian death camp. Somehow, his experience impacted him in such a way that it caused him to write, 'Bless you prison, bless you for being in my life. For there, lying upon the rotting prison straw, I came to realize that the object of life is not prosperity as we are made to believe, but the maturity of the human soul.'[6]

As we talked about earlier, for C.S. Lewis God chose the long sickness and early death of his wife and closest friend, Joy Davidman. In his book about the experience, *The Problem of*

Pain, Lewis says, 'When pain is to be borne, a little courage helps more than much knowledge, a little human sympathy more than much courage, and the least tincture of the love of God more than all.'[7]

God chose to reveal this to me in front of that great seventeenth-century painting and God will choose your moment for you too… that is, if you will let Him.

Where is God?

Richard Rohr says that

The 16th question in the Baltimore Catechism,[8] 'Where is God?' is answered straightforwardly: 'God is everywhere.' The summit of Christian prayer is accomplished when you can trust that you are constantly in the presence of God. You cannot not be in the presence of God! Where would you go? As the psalmist says [Psalm 139:7–9], if you go up to the heavens or underneath the earth, you still can't get away from God. God is either in all things, or God is in nothing. Jesus spent a great deal of his ministry trying to break down the false distinctions between 'God's here' and 'God's not there.' He dared to see God everywhere, even in sin, in enemies, in failures, and in outsiders.[9]

I'm learning that there really are many ways to see or to hear or to know God. There are many ways for Him to step into our journey and to catch us by the arm or to tap us on the shoulder. My desire for each of us, as we share this time together, is that we would each feel the ever-so-gentle tug of our lover-God. And as we seek God and as we ask Him what the journey to healing looks like for our own situation – what to forgive, what we need to let go of and what to learn to thank God for allowing in our lives – let us *be strong and of good courage.*[10] Because while it so very often doesn't feel like it, we have to believe that God is for us and loves us jealously. Until we are willing to lay face down before God and tell Him that our pain is His to take and His to use, however He wants, I am certain that we will never be able to fully experience the freedom or tremendous love that He has in store for us. And without His love fuelling us, we'll never be able to love ourselves or anybody else.

As you throw yourself out into His arms, no matter how narrow the path becomes or how steep the climb, with God the risk is fully worth it! He alone has the power to un-cripple each of us and to lead us by His hand to hope and freedom. God's love eats away at the cancer of bitterness, like 'Light-seeds … planted in the souls of God's people, Joy-seeds … planted in good heart-soil'.[11]

So, what do you think? With God on our side like this, how can we lose? If God didn't hesitate to put everything on the line for us, embracing our condition and exposing himself to the worst by sending his own Son, is there anything else he wouldn't gladly and freely do for us? And who would dare tangle with God by messing with one of God's chosen? Who would dare even to point a finger? The One who died for us – who was raised to life for us! – is in the presence of God at this very moment sticking up for us.

Do you think anyone is going to be able to drive a wedge between us and Christ's love for us? There is no way! Not trouble, not hard times, not hatred, not hunger, not homelessness, not bullying threats, not backstabbing, not even the worst sins listed in Scripture: They kill us in cold blood because they hate you. We're sitting ducks; they pick us off one by one. None of this fazes us because Jesus loves us. I'm absolutely convinced that nothing – nothing living or dead, angelic or demonic, today or tomorrow, high or low, thinkable or unthinkable – absolutely nothing can get between us and God's love because of the way that Jesus our Master has embraced us.[12]

Take Time

In his book *Interior Freedom*, Jacques Philippe reminds us that 'The only way to diminish the suffering that burdens mankind is by forgiveness.'[13] And as we take some time at the end of this chapter, I want you to think about that statement – your forgiving has the power to impact all of humanity. Wow!

But I see it as an extremely personal statement too – your act of forgiving has the power to diminish the suffering that burdens you.

- What is it that you need to forgive, and what do you need to let go of? Do you need to forgive God for not protecting you better? Do you need to forgive others for not stepping in and putting a stop to your pain?
- Are you able yet to thank God for allowing pain in your life?
- These are HUGE questions, so *be strong and of good courage*. God is with you right now in the turbulent waters.

Pray

Teach me, my Lord, to be sweet and gentle in all the events of life … In disappointments, teach me to profit by the suffering that comes across my path. Let me so use it that it may mellow me, not harden or embitter me; that it may make me patient, not irritable; that it may make me broad in my forgiveness … May my life be lived in the supernatural, full of power for good, and strong in its purpose of sanctity … Flood my soul with your spirit and life ... Penetrate and possess my whole being … that every soul I come in contact with may feel your presence in my soul. Let them look up and see no longer me, but only JESUS.[14]

Amen.

Chapter Twelve:
The Bravest Thing

Owning our story and loving ourselves through that process is the bravest thing that we will ever do.[1]
Brené Brown

During the process of researching and writing this book, my wife and I have talked a lot about our own pain and spent plenty of time praying through our own struggles. How to move forward in a way that allows God to continually bring us to wholeness and healing has become the driving force behind so much of what we pray. Through this very intentional process, we're learning to see ourselves the way God sees us and the way He always intended for us to see – with spiritual eyes of love.

One of the biggest things that has helped me almost more than anything else has been discovering the importance of looking at my story (every part of it), as *my* story. It defines who I am today and I need to own that fact; I need to take hold of it and understand that I am who I am because God made me with intention, passion and purpose. He designed my personality, weaknesses and flaws included; He leads me and draws me through the pathways of my life. But He knew we'd struggle with this, and that's why we're reminded constantly throughout the Scriptures to 'Trust in the LORD with all your heart, and do not rely on your own understanding; think about Him in all your ways, and He will guide you on the right paths'.[2]

The Message is even plainer, telling us not to 'try to figure out everything on your own. [Instead we need to] Listen for GOD's voice … He's the one who will keep you on track'.[3]

Prayer should never be used as a plea for God to get rid of the problems in our lives; instead, it should be used as a means to connect with God and to redeem and repair the broken soul. I need to learn how to identify with the person I see in the mirror, and not to *pray* that person away. While it has always been my view, God has shown me through this process that He doesn't require the man in the mirror to be erased and replaced by Christ. When Paul told the Corinthian Church that we would become new creations through Jesus dying on the cross, he wasn't saying that Christ died to blot me out. He died to give us fresh eyes to 'look inside, and what we see is that anyone united with the Messiah gets a fresh start'.[4] And that was what I needed so very badly; I needed to see my situation in a fresh way.

God, please don't take the pain away

I needed to see that God so wants me to fall in love with Him more and more, and then fall even further and more deeply in love with Him. I see now that He keeps pressing me and driving me towards the greener pastures. And He'll keep doing this until I realise that I need to stop running… instead of 'God, please take the memories and the pain away', the prayer of my heart is now a whole lot bigger and a whole lot scarier.

Instead I'm figuring out, with His help and grace, how to 'Love the Lord your God with all your passion and prayer and intelligence'[5] *because* of my past and not despite it.

God works in ways that are so unique and individual, as each of our situations require. He's reaching out His hand to me, to you, and He's asking us to embrace who we are, with our past, including the busted-up, broken, wrecked aspects of our lives and cry out to Him with every drop of pain and passion:

> God, You know best so I give you complete permission – take me; take my past; take my anger; pain and resentment too. Use it all, God, that I may see myself as You see me. Show me, God, how I can spend the rest of this life learning to love You more, and to love myself more, so that I can love others just as much.

Remember, this book is not the *self-contained* answer guaranteed to bring the healing to your busted-up or broken, wrecked past. But it's my prayer that it would be a door of hope that encourages you to press on in the journey that is the rest of your life. But before we dust ourselves off, part ways and set off on that trail again, I want to spend the time during the closing chapters of this book unpacking the 'love God, love others as you love yourself' words of Jesus. They have been the mystical key that has allowed me to explore what it means to embrace *me*, and therefore embrace my pain and anger and hurt. While my awakening hasn't come easily, and while I have agonised over the principles God has been revealing to me, it's the understanding of those words that has proved to be the catalyst behind my own healing and ability to forgive. It's also what has driven me to write this book, which (just for the record) has been the source of some of the greatest challenges of my life. I now believe that it's much easier to leave the lid on life, but you can only get to the heart when you take the risk and lift the lid!

We have spent way too much of our lives searching for a way out, when it was with 'the grace and peace poured into our lives by God our Father and our Master, Jesus Christ,'[6] that we have come to this *very moment*. I have fought this for the longest time, but this day, I declare, 'No more!' No more will I ask God to make new, as in replace the old Tim Sisarich with a different, new Tim Sisarich. Instead, I want to ask God for new eyes to see what He sees when He looks upon me, new ears to hear what He says when He thinks of me, new words to speak of the parts of my life that cause me shame, guilt and agony. God is *not* disappointed with what has happened to the creature that you or I have become, and nor shall we be.

Have a look at how Eugene Peterson so beautifully and poetically articulates these most profound words of Paul, in his letter to the early Ephesian Christians. As you read it, allow the person or event that still causes anguish to your soul to come into your thoughts... allow God to speak to your situation, through these words.

How blessed is God! And what a blessing he is! He's the Father of our Master, Jesus Christ, and takes us to the high places of blessing in him. Long before he laid down earth's foundations, he had us in mind, had settled on us as the focus of his love, to be made whole and holy by his love. Long, long ago he decided to adopt us into his family through Jesus Christ. (What pleasure he took in planning this!) He wanted us to enter into the celebration of his lavish gift-giving by the hand of his beloved Son.

Because of the sacrifice of the Messiah, his blood poured out on the altar of the Cross, we're a free people – free of penalties and punishments chalked up by all our misdeeds. And not just barely free, either. *Abundantly free!* He thought of everything, provided for everything we could possibly need, letting us in on the plans he took such delight in making. He set it all out before us in Christ, a long-range plan in which everything would be brought together and summed up in him, everything in deepest heaven, everything on planet earth.

It's in Christ that we find out who we are and what we are living for.

Long before we first heard of Christ and got our hopes up, he had his eye on us, had designs on us for glorious living, part of the overall purpose he is working out in everything and everyone.

It's in Christ that you, once you heard the truth and believed it (this Message of your salvation), found yourselves home free – signed, sealed, and delivered by the Holy Spirit. This signet from God is the first installment on what's coming, a reminder that we'll get everything God has planned for us, a praising and glorious life.

That's why, when I heard of the solid trust you have in the Master Jesus and your outpouring of love to all the followers of Jesus, I couldn't stop thanking God for you – every time I prayed, I'd think of you and give thanks.

But I do more than thank. I ask – ask the God of our Master, Jesus Christ, the God of glory – to make you intelligent and discerning in knowing him personally, your eyes focused and clear, so that you can see exactly what it is he is calling you to do, grasp the immensity of this glorious way of life he has for his followers, oh, the utter extravagance of his work in us who trust him – endless energy, boundless strength!

All this energy issues from Christ: God raised him from death and set him on a throne in deep heaven, in charge of running the universe, everything from galaxies to governments, no name and no power exempt from his rule. And not just for the time being, but forever. He is in charge of it all, has the final word on everything. At the center of all this, Christ rules the church. The church, you see, is not peripheral to the world; the world is peripheral to the church. The church is Christ's body, in which he speaks and acts, by which he fills everything with his presence.[7]

Paul tells us that God is a blessing to us and that He wants more than *just* to bless us... He wants to take us to the *highest places* of blessing. Though you might not feel it or see it, He has given you life and breath as a gift, and you have to reconcile the fact that where you are and what you have been through, is both part of that gift and essential in God's plan of cracking the shell that surrounds your heart. I know it's hard, but be brave and choose to own your story and open your life before Him, to receive His love.

Not barely free... abundantly free!

Owning your past, instead of running and hiding from it, is the access point through which you will gain the freedom you need to discover and receive God's promised blessing. It will require an act of faith while your head and heart catch up to what God has already made available through Calvary. It will require plenty of prayer; it might require daily journaling and repeating biblical truth; it may require sharing some of your past with others; it may very well require professional counselling to help you understand that you are free to live and love and be loved... As Paul says, 'not just barely free, either. *Abundantly* free!'

When God drew up the plans and map for our individual journeys, according to the writings of Paul and the other biblical writers, the designs were for *glorious living*, and if God is the God of all, then we have to come to a place where, while we may never completely understand His reasons or methods, we accept and find comfort in the reality that every step of the way is somehow part of His overall purpose that He is working out in everything and everyone.

God knows you so deeply and so intimately. Even your best 'poker face' hides nothing from him. He can finish your sentences, before you open your mouth, because he knows you. Nothing gets past him – not your past and the hurts that hide there, not your future and the dreams you've hidden there. He knows what will cause you to fall and what will help you up and make you run. There are things He knows about you that you yourself will never know or understand this side of heaven. And so when God allows you to go through or experience something, perhaps this is the nature of the God whom Christians worship and to whom we have given ourselves. Perhaps He is saying, 'Though you'll never fully understand in this lifetime of yours, trust Me because there is light at the end of this tunnel and I came to seek and save those who were lost, not to rob, steal, betray and destroy.'

What I have a really hard time with as I have reflected on these thoughts is the reality that God's ways *really* aren't our ways! While I said all the right 'faith' words, I somehow figured that I had a grip on who He is and on the way He works. But the fact is that I don't... while I see things dimly now, the time will come that I will eventually see all things as clearly as He does; when the day breaks and the night watch ends, it will be obvious that He never once let me down, that He never once cheated or betrayed me. The rough part, as someone once told me, is that 'Your feelings of rejection and betrayal were actually part of God's plan to get your attention and make you able to better receive His love'.

I wanted to see God swoop in and sweep all the baggage away, but instead I feel like He has come in and 'cleaned house', packed it all up and handed it to me in a travel case. But as He points me back to the path of life, He encourages me to own my story and then hold Him responsible for the solution for all that baggage. And you know if, as the letter to the Ephesians tells us, He is 'in charge of running the universe, everything from galaxies to governments' and that 'no name and no power [is] exempt from his rule', I figure He'd have no issue in giving you the wisdom and ability to know Him for yourself: He would give you spiritual eyes to see His plan and purpose for you, and the absolutely incredible life He has in mind for you.

However, faith is the only indicator that the unseen will one day be seen, the only ingredient that'll bring your hope to life. So before God can fill you with the ability to change, to love, to heal, you have to choose to believe and have faith that it is actually possible. I'm not implying it is an easy *next step*, yet that's no reason or justification not to take it. It's not a reason not to fight for healing, to pursue forgiveness, to sell all so that you can be well. As hard as it may be to get a grip of this point, we must come to the realisation that nothing is wasted in God's economy of things. God has shown me that my journey, with all the potholes, pitfalls and train wrecks, is part of something much bigger and more beautiful than I could ever see or imagine right now. The same is true for you too.

Archbishop Desmond Tutu articulated it beautifully in *The Book of Forgiving*, speaking of the twenty-seven years that Nelson Mandela spent locked away in an eight by seven foot prison cell on Robben Island. He writes:

When people say to me what a waste it was, I say no, it was not a waste. It took twenty-seven years for him to be transformed from an angry, unforgiving young radical into an icon of reconciliation, forgiveness, and honour who could go on to lead a country back from the brink of civil war and self-destruction.[8]

Bishop Tutu reminds me that God wrote my story and He drew the map for my life long before even the earth was formed. My past is part of that story and today I need to acknowledge that the fingerprints of God, the Master Designer, are on *all* things, and embrace all of my life as a gift from Him.

Take Time

Owning your journey and acknowledging that nothing is random or without reason are such crucial steps to a deep and complete healing. It may be that it's not until God wraps up this life and you stand before Him in heaven that He'll reveal the masterpiece that you are. So while it may make absolutely no sense to you now, when that day comes you will see that the whole of your existence is a gift from Him.

- So let's take some time now to process that concept. Are you willing to own your past? Are you willing to acknowledge that you are free? 'And not just barely free, either', but '*Abundantly free*'? Do you accept that God is 'in charge of running the universe, everything from galaxies to governments' and that 'no name and no power [is] exempt from his rule'? And if you can concede that, then are you willing to also concede that your feeling of being let down by Him is part of His strange yet holy plan to get your attention?

• Are you prepared right now to put your hand in the strong hand of God and say, with David, from Psalm 19, 'the life-maps of GOD are right ... The decisions of GOD are accurate'[9]? Do you think you can do that? To help you take this step forward, why don't you pray with me?

Pray

God, I acknowledge that You are in charge of it all, that You have the final word on everything. God, I acknowledge that You know best, so I give You complete permission to take me; take my past; take my anger, pain and resentment too. Use it all, God, that I may see myself as You see me.

Long before You laid down the earth's foundations, you had me in mind and you settled on me as the focus of your love; you have made me holy with your love. Because of the sacrifice of the Messiah, His blood poured out on the altar of the cross, I am free ... completely and abundantly free!!

Even though I can't see it right now, You thought of everything, provided for everything I could possibly need. You have always had Your eye on me, had designs on me for glorious living... I am part of the overall purpose You are working out in everything and everyone.

God, in faith I declare that I believe in your contract promise, signed with Christ's blood on the cross, that I will get everything God has planned for me – a praising and glorious life. Give me energy and strength; help my eyes to be focused and clear, so that I can see exactly what it is You are calling me to do: to grasp the immensity of this glorious life that you have given me.[10]

Amen.

Chapter Thirteen:
God Loves Us As We Are

I thank you, High God – you're breathtaking!
Body and soul, I am marvelously made![1]
Psalm 139 (The Message)

The big issue I have with choosing the *God-is-the-author-of-my-life* route is that it really leaves me with only one option with the circumstances that I find myself in – that God wrote them. The One who loves me with the purest, most stunning and luxuriously extravagant love is the One who jotted down every word on every page. God's hand *wrote* the episodes that make up the story of my life, and He has His reasons for the storyline – to bless and not to harm.

The biggest temptation with pain that I've personally found is allowing ourselves to feel like the world is against us or that it's just too unfair... we need pity. But if God is our author, then when we cast blame and demand pity it's really just veiled anger at God. There is no easy way to write these words, so I won't. I will very uncourageously defer to a man older, wiser and more learned than me – R.T. Kendall. He writes:

Self-pity gets us nowhere with God. Absolutely nowhere. As James put it, 'our wrath does not work the righteousness of God.' (James 1:20, KJV). We may wish that our sulking and hurt might move God to feel pity for us. It doesn't work that way. As long as we are feeling sorry for ourselves and are hoping this will make God sorry for what He allowed in our lives, dream on! I wish it weren't so, but self-pity does not make God say, 'I'm so sorry for allowing you to go through this,' as if He owes us an apology. Self-pity is our unsubtle attempt to manipulate God. He doesn't fall for it. As Joseph refused to let his brothers feel distress over what they did, so we too must set God totally free by refusing to try and make Him feel He has wronged us. Don't go there. Don't even think it![2]

The God of the Bible is the Creator of the universe and the ruler of heaven and earth. And it is that God who created you and loved you. He loved you long before anything or anyone was made. You are no accident, and your life has always been in His hand. God has been very purposeful with everything that has happened in your life; it didn't catch Him by surprise or happen while He was having an afternoon snooze. The opposite is true – everything that has happened to you and everything that you have experienced has purpose and value in the story of your life. That means I have to look back though those chapters and search those reasons out, search for Him on every page. What makes that harder than it might look on paper is that the healing process isn't a carefully laid out and well-worn path to freedom; it is a series of steps, a process, an ongoing walk through life. God has specifically carved the path-to-healing that I am travelling with Him, and it will quite likely be different from yours. And we have to go there with Him.

With all your heart, soul and mind
I do not want to belittle your past nor the pain that may litter it,

but you and I both need to hear these words: it is time to choose to believe the truth and refuse to be blinded by lies. I have seen and cannot deny that God has a purpose in everything. He permits all that happens to me, and the reason for that is deeply rooted in an overwhelming love for me. And that truth is yours to own too. Healing begins with God and ends with God, and that's why Jesus said that the greatest commandment is to love God. If I want to see the remaining chapters of *The Book of Me* filled with hope and joy rather than with more confusion and darkness, I have to throw all caution to the wind and to do everything I can to find out how I can bless the Lord, not just for the good days but for *all* He has done in my life.

I need to set my GPS to that place where I can thank God for my life and then I need to spend the trip focusing on celebrating that every aspect of it is both God-breathed and God-purposed. How does anyone do that, especially when the pages of life might fail to make sense in light of all the 'rise up on wings like eagles'-type verses in the Bible? Well, when Jesus was asked the question, He replied that you do it 'with all your heart, with all your soul, and with all your mind'.[3] Or as *The Message* puts it, 'with all your passion and prayer and intelligence'.[4]

The German pastor Dietrich Bonhoeffer was an incredible man. Aside from his amazing teachings and writings, he was a man who had to grapple with what loving God 'with all your passion, prayer and intelligence' looked like in the chaotic world of Second World War Germany. All around him, people were being carted away simply for being Jewish, gypsy, mentally ill, or gay. Because of his involvement in the failed plot to assassinate Adolf Hitler, Bonhoeffer was arrested and imprisoned by the Gestapo. Just three weeks before Hitler's suicide and the German surrender to Allied forces, the thirty-nine-year-old pastor was executed on charges of treason against the Führer.

While his faith and strength of character are both amazing examples to any Christian, his is not the story I want us to focus on here. For that, I'd recommend *Bonhoeffer: A Biography* by Eric Metaxas (Thomas Nelson). I want to draw your attention to another from this same time. Three short years before his death, in June 1942, Dietrich Bonhoeffer met and fell in love with eighteen-year-old Maria von Wedemeyer. Not a whole lot is written about this young woman or of her relationship with Bonhoeffer. That is, apart from a handful of letters that she kept hidden for most of her life. She'd been 'repeatedly urged'[5] to release the letters for publication, but it appears that these were the one part of Dietrich Bonhoeffer she wanted to keep private. However, in 1977, a year before she died, she gave all the letters to her sister, giving her permission to make known to the world the words that had been locked in her own heart for so long – a task that took her sister fifteen years to complete.

As you read the letters, you see the reality of a young woman so deeply in love with a man, telling him, 'Dear, Beloved Dietrich, … I doubt there's an hour in the day when my thoughts don't turn to you … it's good to feel you're near … I am in love with every sentence, every word, every squiggle of your hand …'

And yet, we also hear her anguish as she grappled with the fact that her lover was heart-crushingly out of reach. 'My hopes, which always scale the heights overnight, go crashing down into a deeper abyss every day' she tells him, '… my heart is in complete turmoil … utterly torn again … if only I could see you.'

If only I could see you

Through it all, the teenage Maria von Wedemeyer clings to her faith and somehow finds a way to love God, despite every reason not to. Within a year of leaving high school and meeting Bonhoeffer, Maria lost her father and brother to the war (they were officers in the German army and both died fighting *against* the Allies). While she was grieving for them, she became engaged to Bonhoeffer, who was arrested soon after… her fiancé was charged with being a traitor to his country and to the very cause for which her father and brother had so recently given their lives. And yet it was this young girl who would become the hand of God, strengthening the man who (through his books and messages) has strengthened so many others since his untimely death. She would constantly be encouraging him, 'Don't get tired and depressed, my dearest Dietrich, it won't be much longer now.'

In a letter to his parents, Bonhoeffer wrote, 'The way she [Maria] copes with everything is a miracle.' To Maria – amongst pleas of, 'Wait with me, I beg you! Let me embrace you long and tenderly, let me kiss you and love you and stroke the sorrow from your brow' – he is constantly praying that God would preserve her strength.[6]

And as I mentioned, very little is written of her, but when I was writing this chapter, her story became one of real value to me. What was it about this woman, and what was it about her faith and love for God that allowed her to stand so strong when, as Bonhoeffer wrote to her, 'This is turning into a wait whose outward purpose I fail to understand, and whose inward purpose has to be re-discovered daily.'

Maria von Wedemeyer was a woman who had every reason to be furious with God. Obviously, she never did marry Dietrich Bonhoeffer, nor would she see him alive again. In fact, she spent four months after the war searching prisons and concentration camps in a frantic bid to find the man who was to be her husband. It took that long for the news of his death to filter down to her.

And despite her prayer-covered and faith-filled upbringing, Maria's journey was not lived 'rising up on wings like eagles'. Along with losing her father and brother to a war they didn't even believe in, and losing her fiancé to a cause that he did believe in, she also had, amongst life's other challenges, two failed marriages and her life snatched from her after her body was devastated by cancer, when she was just fifty-three.

And yet this is the part I love most about unearthing her story – unlike Dietrich Bonhoeffer, who is so often seen as the face of Christian strength, faith and character during the war, whose life is told and retold through books, movies and countless articles, and who now has Foundations and Libraries named after him, Maria von Wedemeyer is a person much like the rest of us – left to live out her life in the shadows. She stands like a beacon of light and encouragement to me because, in the face of such immense pain, she didn't give up on God and she didn't give up on life. It would appear that instead of letting her experiences drain the life out of her, she chose instead to let the cracks and streaks of heartbreak be used by God as a source of strength and blessing, a trait we hear in her words to Bonhoeffer near the end of his life: 'As long as there is something to look forward to, one should always be thankful.'[7]

From the little that I could find out about her, I found that she packed a lot of thankfulness into that short time. In the historical notes of *Love Letters from Cell 92*, we're told that 'She cared for people more than the problems, so she solved the problems' to make life better for those around her. 'The number of people who were at [her] funeral – and the kind of people [who attended] – attests to that.' The spotlight of history might have missed this, but Bonhoeffer didn't, writing in a letter to her, 'You don't write books, fortunately; you *do, know, learn*, and *fill with real life* that which I have only dreamed of.'[8]

God handpicked you!

There are thousands of stories just like this one that colour human history with hope and purpose. I have chosen just one, of a young woman who would allow God the room to cause her to thrive. Her life is a beautiful reminder to me that I can be included amongst those whom heaven smiles over because of how I live my life. And so can you. It really doesn't matter how your story or journey brought you to this place today. Paul tells us through his letter to the Corinthian church that 'God deliberately chose men and women that the culture overlooks, exploits and abuses: He chose these "nobodies". Everything that we have, Paul says, 'comes from God'.[9]

Just like Maria von Wedemeyer was chosen by God to live a life that I'd be willing to bet she never imagined or even wished for as a child, God handpicked you! He handpicked you to be the recipient of His unending, unfathomable, unquenchable, breathtaking love, and He chose to reveal Himself and His love to you in and through your experiences – every single one of them.

Take Time

We opened this chapter with a verse from Psalm 139. It is a declaration of the wonderment of God in the creation of each one of us. The psalmist is staggered at how marvellously made we are, body and soul. He saw that the road to his future was paved in faith; he chose to proclaim that God was incredible in the way He shaped and formed both body and soul, and he did this with all his passion, prayer and intelligence.

- As we take some time now, I'd encourage you to ponder that verse and think about it in the light of your own experiences. Are you still struggling to acknowledge that you are marvellously made? That God handpicked you, for the life that you are living? Do you still find it hard to see that your soul or your personality, emotions and humanity are all marvellously made and shaped by God? Spend some time processing that with God.

- Now think for a moment about what we have just read about Maria von Wedemeyer and her words, 'As long as there is something to look forward to, one should always be thankful.' Can you be thankful for what God has put in your 'lap'?

- When you're ready, take all those feelings and thoughts to God. Go to Him with all your heart, soul and mind.

Pray

Oh God, R.T. Kendall's words are hard – that self-pity is my unsubtle attempt to manipulate You. I have longed for you to fix my situation, or at least tell me You're sorry for allowing me to go through this. Today I choose to refuse to block the way you have carved out for me. God, I proclaim and confess that You have handpicked me to be the beneficiary of Your unending, unfathomable, unquenchable, breathtaking love. And I choose to not only accept but praise You for the ways You reveal Yourself and Your love to me in and through my life's experiences – every single one of them.

Amen.

Chapter Fourteen:
Start Here

~

We have to start in the same place: I am worthy.[1]
Brené Brown

Jesus tells us in the Gospels that He came, not to take away a single word that God spoke through the wise men and women of the Old Testament, but that He came to fulfil them – see, for example, Matthew 5:17. And, as we have already talked about, when He was asked to pinpoint the most important of those teachings, He gave us that incredibly brief statement, the statement that we'll be directing our gaze to during these closing chapters.

> Jesus said, 'Love the Lord your God with all your passion and prayer and intelligence.' This is the most important, the first on any list. But there is a second to set alongside it: 'Love others as well as you love yourself.' These two commands are pegs; everything in God's Law and the Prophets hangs from them.'[2]

Jesus, God in the flesh, declares that all of the words of the Law and the Prophets in the Old Testament hang on that one single statement of *loving God and loving others as much as you love yourself.*

It's pretty safe to assume that a declaration like that, from

God Himself, is kind of important, right? We should pay careful attention to His words and we should invest all of our heart and soul into trying to understand and know those words; we should wake up every day with the single-minded goal to live this day in a way that fulfils those words.

As I've journeyed through both the valleys and the meadows, the dark forests and the awe-inspiring hilltops of this life of mine, I've found that the hardest part of the whole *loving God, loving others as I love myself* statement of God is the *love myself* bit, as I have mentioned before. I realise that I'm never going to fully understand God, yet I have always (to the best of my understanding) sought to love Him, serve Him and honour Him. I also understand the importance of loving others and making them feel that they are made in God's image; that they are special and loved by Him. I have really tried to live in a way that helped them see that too. Although, in the writing of this book I have understood that that is not completely true – there are some I have filed away into the *too painful* basket. Writing has helped me immeasurably with that because it has forced me to confront my feelings and thoughts, and challenged me to deal with my demons before moving on.

Got to find love

That said, the one thing I have always had the most trouble with is the loving of me. I know me; I know every sin I have ever acted out, every sin I have thought out, and every sin I am capable of. I know how much of my life is built on sticks and straw; and I know how much of who I am is nothing but bluff and bluster. I have always felt that being selfless and self-sacrificing was a far safer way to live, as opposed to having the light of truth turned on, and having the *real* me being humiliated in front of others.

Radio is the greatest career for people like me – I get to create my 'on-air' persona, hide behind the microphone, and no one ever has to meet the real man, who feels like a fraud anyway.

The utter tragedy is that all of that claptrap is self-imposed. All those sorts of feelings come from within my own fallen and frail humanity. That's not God's mind at all. The difficulty with this kind of thinking is that it very quickly becomes a very slippery slope into a whirlpool of misery. There we spin round and round, somehow feeling like all the sin we have done has opened the window to allow all the pain into our lives, that it's all somehow our fault. I have discovered that I was drowning in a pool of shame that I had built myself, and the walls were reinforced by others speaking into my life in ways that just weren't healthy. And the more I struggled, the deeper I sank, and it was breaking God's heart!

I couldn't comprehend the reality of the closing paragraph in the previous chapter: that God handpicked each one of us; that God calls each of us to learn to love Him and that He calls us to learn to *be loved* by Him. This battle for the *love of me* is the single biggest roadblock to the path of a hope-filled future. It is not until we get to that place of not simply understanding in our heads, but fully realising with all our being, that we are loved and that we need to love every facet of our selves – the shame, the pain… everything – that we will be free to *know* Him, *learn* of Him, and be *filled* with Him. And when that happens, I now realise that it empowers us to be filled with His love and grace for others.

I thank God that He has torn open the veil of the Temple, through Christ's work on the cross. That act has allowed each one of us the immeasurable benefit of seeing the *real* heart and face of God for ourselves. The God-Man has given us a way to be free from the choking grip of the self-induced lie of never measuring up to some twisted, human understanding of the God-standard. Jesus has given us the way to be free from the power of sin, the grip of pain and from the fear of death. Through His agony and through the pouring out of his blood, we are now able to drink in to the fullest extent, the love that has been given to us so unconditionally by a Father who loves us for who we are, just as we are, right where we are. He doesn't wait till we are free of our faults and failing, but loves us with all that bundled in. God has already reached out to us; He already loves us, right where we're at.

The key to freedom

He tells us that the key to unlock this understanding is not in lofty theological wisdom or in some forced, grovelling humility; the key to your freedom and mine, from the grip of a past that Satan continues to use as a brick to batter us with, is the way we feel about ourselves.

If you think about this practically, how are we expected to ever feel accepted by others, let alone God, when we have set a standard for ourselves that is so impossibly high? It's our choice if we want to remove all that blinds, so we can see and experience that love in our lives as we walk into a hope-filled future.

The reality check here is that there's no way any of us will be able to truly love God or love others or forgive others, for that matter, until we come to terms with who *we are*. We are loved by God, designed by God and created as an image and reflection of him to the world around us. And yes, this might be an incredibly hard idea to chew and digest, to apply to your own life. I find it so hard to love *me* or to even see why God would love me. Instead of making it my purpose and my goal to understand the heart of God where I was concerned, I just kind of gave up. I thought if I could concentrate on the other two (loving God and loving others), then that just might be enough to get me over the finishing line and to make it into the 'well done, good and faithful servant'[3] queue.

But that's not what God called me to, and it's not what He wants for you either. James Martin, drawing on the very profound writings of Thomas Merton, put it this way:

God has made each of us uniquely ourselves, and holiness consists of discovering the true self, the person we are before God, accepting that person … In the quest for the true self, one therefore begins to appreciate and accept one's personality and one's life as an essential way that God calls us to be ourselves.[4]

As we travel the road to healing and forgiveness, we must find a way to see ourselves as beautiful, delightful and the apple, or *the one in the very centre*, of God's eye. No matter what happened *to* you, or what happened *through* you, for healing to come, you have to start with believing that you are worthy of love, acceptance and grace… each of us needs to be able to say, with conviction, 'I am worthy!' Without that, none of us will ever be able to unlock all the secret rooms in our lives, the ones that we've jammed all the *too painful* baskets into.

Summarising the theologian Walter Kasper, from his book Jesus the Christ, if we are to ever genuinely experience and understand God's love for us, and through His love, learn to love Him back, as well as love those around us, especially if they have caused us grief and pain, we have to allow ourselves to fully comprehend the fact that each one of us has been unreservedly accepted, approved and infinitely loved by God; that we can and should accept ourselves that way.[5]

Genuine freedom doesn't come through choosing to love God or through accepting Christ as our Saviour. That is a huge step in the right direction, but the greatest eye-opener for us is when we reach that place of knowing beyond any shadow of doubt that we are unconditionally loved and accepted by God, just as we are.

Your wounds don't define you

That realisation came for me, not like the switching on of a light or like a sudden flood, but more like the gentle and quiet opening of a delicate little flower bud. Drop by agonising drop, as I have knelt at the foot of the cross, the blood of Christ has slowly and gently cleansed my wounds and washed the blinding lies from my eyes. As part of that process, I stumbled upon the writings and teachings of a man by the name of Brennan Manning.

Manning was a man who definitely tussled with that concept of truly loving himself, and with great reason. Born and raised in Brooklyn, New York during the Great Depression, Manning seemed to have a hard time with who he was and where he fitted in. He managed a semester of journalism at university, then figured the Marines might be an easier path to growing up. But when that didn't work out for him, he floundered around until a spiritual director suggested the priesthood.

That led him to become a Franciscan monk, serving the poor across the world. In France, he worked as a kitchen-hand, washing dishes; in Switzerland, he spent time in prison so he could act as a prison chaplain to a group of men who had none. The only person who knew of his reasons for being there and of his innocence was the prison warden, who allowed him to live amongst the prisoners as one of them. In Spain, he spent six months in some remote cave. After returning to the US, he had a monumental collapse into alcoholism that so swallowed him up that he ended up walking away from the priesthood and living on the streets, drinking anything that would keep him from becoming sober. He tried marriage, and loved his wife, but the love and tug for another drink proved stronger. The alcoholism never left him, but became his constant shadow. He would wrestle with it his entire life and it was the effects of the alcoholism that eventually killed him. Brennan Manning died in April 2013.

But it wasn't the alcoholism that defined this man. Nor was it any of the long list of failures that defined him either. Brennan Manning was defined and will be forever remembered as a man who lived his life desperately clutching hold of the cloak of Christ. His message, unchanged for more than fifty years, was so incredibly simple, yet strangely hard to catch a hold of:

God loves you unconditionally, as you are and not as you should be, because nobody is as they should be. It is the message of grace … a grace that amazes as it offends. A grace that pays the eager beaver who works all day long the same wages as the grinning drunk who shows up at ten to five. A grace that hikes up the robe and runs breakneck toward the prodigal who is reeking of sin, and wraps him up and decides to throw a party with no ifs or buts. A grace that raises bloodshot eyes to a dying thief's request – 'Please remember me' –and assures him, 'You bet!' … It works without asking anything of us. It's not cheap. It's free, and as such will always be a banana peel for the orthodox foot and a fairy tale for the grown-up sensibility. Grace is sufficient even though we huff and puff with all our might to try to find something or someone it cannot cover. Grace is enough. He is enough. Jesus is enough.[6]

As I pored over his writings and as I heard his anguish and affliction of soul, I heard God speak to *my* broken and bruised heart. For the first time in my life, I heard and caught that simple yet life-quaking truth that God loves me.

Unshakable and unwavering

That truth was and will always be like water to my sorry soul. It will always be the first rung of the ladder that God drops into my pit of despair. We all need to grab that first rung as if our very life depended on it. When we do, 'In unshaken trust, unwavering hope, and the pure giving of love,' Manning wrote in *The Wisdom of Tenderness*:

> we hand over the kingdom of ourselves to the Father. And the Abba, the Daddy of Jesus, standing on the eternal shores with open, outstretched arms, gently beckons us home, saying, Come now, my love, my lovely one, come, For you the winter is past, The snows are over and gone. The flowers appear in the land, The season of joyful songs has come …. Come now, my love, my lovely one, come, … Let me see your face, Let me hear your voice. For your voice is sweet and your face so beautiful. Come now, my love, my lovely one, come.[7]

What gives me such hope about this is that it was through all of the life-shattering experiences that rocked his world that Brennan Manning discovered this for himself. It wasn't when he was soaring on *wings like eagles*, but it was when he was lying in a gutter. It was in the pain, and it was because of the pain that this broken man got a glimpse of the furious longing of God. When he had absolutely nothing to offer, he was able to hear his *Abba* say:

Don't wait until you have your act cleaned up and your head on straight. Don't delay until you think you are properly disposed and free of pride and lust, jealousy and self-hatred. Come to me in your brokenness and sinfulness, with all your fears and insecurities, and I will comfort you. I will come to you right where you live and love you just the way you are, and not the way you think you should be.[8]

Take Time

- When we *let God in*, and give Him the room to wrap us in His arms of love, it changes us. It allows us to learn to love ourselves, which was His plan all along. And I'm starting to understand just how central that idea of learning to love ourselves, learning to love myself, is to attain that most beautiful freedom in Christ, promised to us in the Gospels – 'if the Son sets you free, you really will be free'.[9]
- As we take some time right now to think through that, sit with those words for a while. Allow yourself the time for them to transform from mere words into holy seeds planted deep within your heart. Even though you might still be smothered in shame or guilt or anger or any other emotion in that long list of hopelessness that Satan has been heaping upon every one of us since Adam and Eve ate the fruit in Eden, I pray that right now you will start to grasp hold of the truth that you are loved and free; free to love and free to live!

Pray

God, I believe in your promises! Your promise of a life free of sin, guilt and death is just the most exquisite thought. Help me believe in faith that You will do just as You have promised. In faith I declare, in the name of Jesus, 1 Corinthians 15 over my life: 'Death [is] swallowed by triumphant Life! ... in a single victorious stroke of Life, all three – sin, guilt, death – are gone ...'[10] Help me never to look at my life as a failure again, nor to accept anything throughout my life as dumb luck or happenstance. You love me and use all things to draw me into a freedom in You. I am worthy and I choose to no longer live under the power of shame. I repent of that right now. And from this day, I pledge to live my days learning to love You, love others and love me.

Thank You and Amen.

Chapter Fifteen:
Be Free!

We all want to be free of the pain of living with a broken and unforgiving heart.[1]
Archbishop Desmond Tutu

We need to grab hold of those final thoughts from the last chapter with both hands, as we dive right into probably the most complicated of the three-part statement of Christ (love God and love others in the same way that you love yourself), and that is these two words – *love others*. I say complicated because, for each one of us, there is so much personal history, memories and emotion tied to the *others* in our lives. When Christ uttered that phase, was He really thinking about me? Was He aware of *all* the people who have impacted my life? Did He see me standing in front of Rembrandt's 'The Return of the Prodigal Son', coming to terms with loving my own dad? I know that I'm not the only person to have stumbled under the burden of these questions, either – people were asking Jesus when He walked the earth who they were to love and forgive.

It's why the message behind the Bible story of the Good Samaritan is so powerful. There's no 'out' clause. Jesus says that we're to forgive everyone; help everyone; love everyone. He left no room for some sort of holy hatred that seems so deserving and appropriate when you consider the people behind human slave trading or Nazi Germany, the Rwandan genocide, Cambodia's Killing Fields… I could go on and on. Jesus makes it plain through that simple little parable that no matter how horrific or genuinely heart-wrenching the stories, God commanded us to *love others*. Who are these *others*? Jesus calls us to love anyone and everyone – no matter who they are and no matter what they have done, love them.

As harsh as that sounds, if Jesus said it, I must choose to find a way to do it. If that seems impossible, then I need to allow God to do whatever He needs to do in me for me to get to the place where I can join Job, who

fell to the ground and worshiped, saying:

Naked I came from my mother's womb,
and naked I will leave this life.
The LORD gives, and the LORD takes away.
Praise the name of Yahweh.[2]

Pain is part of life's tapestry

While I might not have experienced what you have experienced or been through what you have had to endure, I have had glimpses. And as I researched for this book, I have been given access to the heart-closeted secrets and stories of literally hundreds of men and women who have horror and tragedy woven all through the tapestry of their lives. It truly is an ugly world, but as we have read already, God loves each one of us so much and He wants us to be free to live life in the fullness of that love. To get to that place, we must learn to love; we must choose to love. The final sentence of Job 1 is an incredible example to us of this: 'Throughout all this Job did not sin or blame God for anything.'[3]

I know that the path to 'the love chapter' in 1 Corinthians is well worn. But it's for good reason. The words are not just beautiful and poetic, they are also truth. As you read them, think about them in the light of your situation.

If I speak human or angelic languages
but do not have love,
I am a sounding gong or a clanging cymbal.
If I have the gift of prophecy
and understand all mysteries
and all knowledge,
and if I have all faith
so that I can move mountains
but do not have love, I am nothing.
And if I donate all my goods to feed the poor,
and if I give my body in order to boast[a]
but do not have love, I gain nothing.
Love is patient, love is kind.
Love does not envy,
is not boastful, is not conceited,
does not act improperly,
is not selfish, is not provoked,
and does not keep a record of wrongs.
Love finds no joy in unrighteousness
but rejoices in the truth.
It bears all things, believes all things,
hopes all things, endures all things.
Love never ends.
But as for prophecies,
they will come to an end;
as for languages, they will cease;

as for knowledge, it will come to an end.
For we know in part,
and we prophesy in part.
But when the perfect comes,
the partial will come to an end.
When I was a child,
I spoke like a child,
I thought like a child,
I reasoned like a child.
When I became a man,
I put aside childish things.
For now we see indistinctly, as in a mirror,
but then face to face.
Now I know in part,
but then I will know fully,
as I am fully known.
Now these three remain:
faith, hope, and love.
But the greatest of these is love.[4]

Is it possible to love, and to love *extravagantly* the ones whose only *gift* to us is a life of tortured memories? Jesus says we can! He did it Himself as He hung on the cross, crying out for God to forgive those who had brutalised Him and who would kill Him. It's really hard for me to jump up and down in joy about this, but there are times and seasons when God *wants* us to be disillusioned with our life. God doesn't want us living in the bubble of an illusion; instead, He wants us to learn to accept the truth that as long as we have breath in our lungs we will 'continue to experience difficulties'.[5]

What God has been showing me is that the secret to this is

how we choose to deal with those difficulties. Yes, damage has been done and things will never go back to the way they were. God doesn't want walls or barriers put up, so that we become entrenched; He wants us walking forward, towards Him. But as long as we hide from the truth of the pain and past through illusions of 'it's all OK, mate' or 'I just lay it at the feet of Jesus' while never actually accepting that what has happened is part of who we are; part of the beautiful person God has created, the devil will use that past and pain to suck us back into the great illusion of a false smile. That's what it really means to become *dis*-illusioned… it is the disestablishment of the illusion.

I will never forget the moment I discovered this – I was talking with my counsellor, sharing about how I was becoming very disillusioned with my faith and my walk with Jesus. I was struggling over the concepts of this book and the realisation that God is Lord over the good and the bad. It was his response that threw me.

'That's fantastic, how does it feel?'

'How does what feel, that I'm questioning everything I've ever believed in?'

'No, how does it feel now the illusion is gone, and you are free to form an unadulterated image of what it means to be a Christian? How does that feel, Tim?'

I know it sounds crazy

It's actually a pretty scary place to be, having your preconceptions obliterated and then having to inch your way through the rubble of what was a worldview. But my counsellor was right about one thing – I was now free of the poisonous illusion that my Christian life would somehow be pain-free. That allowed me to take a really honest look at my life and accept what God had done with me was good.

Acceptance doesn't take away or excuse what happened, but it will lead us to a place where we can see the solution more clearly – and that solution is the immensely powerful tool of forgiveness. In his somewhat autobiographical novel, Gregory David Roberts said that for him, he knew that he had two choices, 'to hate them or to forgive them. And … I don't know why, or how, but it was absolutely clear to me that I had to forgive them. I had to, if I wanted to survive. I know it sounds crazy.'[6]

Roberts is right, it does sound crazy. But what is equally true is that the only real way to take the suffering from our lives is to become disillusioned with the status quo and give room for the power of forgiveness to have its way in us.

The hour and a half I spent with Izzeldin Abuelaish still stands out in my mind as one of the most powerful and memorable radio interviews of the twenty-plus years I've spent in the media. I was first introduced to Dr Abuelaish and his tragic story via a YouTube video that opens with an Israeli news reporter in the middle of a live TV broadcast. His phone rings and he decides to answer it. The clip shows the reporter sitting there, listening in abject horror as Izzeldin Abuelaish screams into the phone, 'They shelled my house. They killed my daughters. Oh God, they killed my daughters. I wanted to save them, but they are dead. They were hit in the head. They died on the spot …'

What I had just witnessed was a Palestinian man struggling to cope with a father's worst nightmare, and it was unfolding live on Israeli TV – three of his daughters and one of his nieces had been blown to bits by the accidental shelling of his home by an Israeli army tank during one of the many wars and skirmishes between the Palestinians and the Israelis.

There was a monstrous explosion that seemed to be all around us, and a thundering, fulminating sound that penetrated my body as though it were coming from within me. I remember the sound. I remember the blinding flash. Suddenly it was pitch-dark, there was dust everywhere, something was sucking the air out of me, I was suffocating ... The sight in front of me was something I hope no other person ever has to witness ... The apartment was full of the dead and wounded ... I wondered who could help us, who could get us out of this catastrophe.[7]

The days and weeks that followed must have been excruciatingly challenging, coming to terms with the agony of loss and then trying to figure out how to keep going, how to continue being a dad to his other children. And from that darkest of days, Dr Izzeldin Abuelaish's story unfolds in a book I'd highly recommend, called *I Shall Not Hate*.

Despite having every reason to hate and to hold on to that hate – born and raised in poverty and the relentless suffering of an overcrowded refugee camp in Gaza, having to learn to live some sort of normal life in the midst of wars and rumours of wars, then his wife and the mother of his eight children dying of leukaemia just months before his daughters' lives were brutally snatched from him – Dr Abuelaish's cry to a world was not for blood or for justice. Instead, incredibly, he was able to tell the world that the answer to overcoming the pain, anger and grief comes only through forgiveness and through love.

While he openly shares that there were definitely times when he hated his life – the misery, filth and poverty – he realised that he, like Gregory David Roberts, also had the same two options to choose from: the path of darkness or the path of light. He chose the way of light, the way of life, writing:

I am not a prophet; I'm a human being and a believer who is trying to accept that what happened to my family was God's plan. The perpetrator was man, the violence man-made, but surely my mission is to try my hardest to ensure that the consequences lead to good, not to ever-increasing evil, violence, and despair ... Tragedy cannot be the end of our lives. We cannot allow it to control and defeat us.[8]

Tragedy cannot be the end

I love that. But it also staggers me... in the face of his overwhelming torment, this man found a way to make the choice of using his pain and brokenness as a means to love even more deeply, because: 'All the desire for revenge and hatred does is drive away wisdom, increase sorrow, and prolong strife.'[9] His life is a true example of Christ's words from Luke 6, to love your enemies and see their blows as an opportunity for God to use them to bring out the best in you, not the worst. And if we can do the same, Jesus tells us:

> You'll never – I promise – regret it. Live out this God-created identity the way our Father lives toward us, generously and graciously, even when we're at our worst. Our Father is kind; you be kind. Don't pick on people, jump on their failures, criticize their faults – unless, of course, you want the same treatment. Don't condemn those who are down; that hardness can boomerang. Be easy on people; you'll find life a lot easier. Give away your life; you'll find life given back, but not merely given back – given back with bonus and blessing.[10]

But, unfortunately so many of us choose the illusion of safety that comes from locking our past in the basement and hiding our pain under the sofa. Unless we learn to find the freedom that can only come from the free fall of God-inspired disillusionment, we'll never have the capacity to allow forgiveness the freedom to saturate our soul. That is the key to unlocking our hearts from the prison of our own bitterness.

Forgiveness is ultimately an act of love, an imitation of what Jesus did for us on the cross, bringing freedom to the person who victimised us. But, according to Archbishop Tutu:

> it also frees the one who forgives. The one who offers forgiveness as a grace is immediately untethered from the yoke that bound him or her to the person who caused the harm. When you forgive, you are free to move on in life, to grow, to no longer be a victim. When you forgive, you slip the yoke, and your future is unshackled from your past.[11]

When we choose to forgive and to love, we are choosing freedom! That freedom is what will enable us to truly be all that God made us to be, complete with an unquenchable hope and a future. That is what Christ came to die for, and what He comes to give us now.

Take Time

I'll share a few final thoughts for our last 'Take Time'. I'd ask you to think very carefully about your life and how you look at it. When I sat down to start this book, my desire was to share how to navigate through the debris of pain, to help rebuild broken relationships. As I wrote in chapter three, I am certain that God is trying to awaken each of us to the hard-to-chew reality that if we don't allow him to *turn our hearts* and to bring us to a place of healing, where the pain-makers in our lives are concerned, the Bible says that we're actually bringing a curse on ourselves.[12]

When it comes to your life, your hurt and the giver of that hurt, I hear God saying:

I am your guide on this journey. I made the path you are walking on. I see a much bigger picture… the secret is that you have to trust that I know what is best for you. I will lead you in that best way, if you would trust Me and let Me lead you. I will use your life and I will use your past and your pain for your good… just as I have always done.

Each of us stand before two paths – the path of darkness and the path of light; choose the path of light and you choose the way to life where you'll find genuine healing and God's power to forgive. As we just read, Luke 6:35-38 reminds us that if you and I choose to walk through it, we won't regret it. I quoted it at the end of chapter 15 from *The Message*, but I suggest you grab your favourite Bible translation and spend a few minutes meditating on those four verses yourself.

Pray

God of mercy, I have read the words and I hear what You have been speaking to me through this book. I acknowledge that You create the path and lead me where I need to go. Like Gregory David Roberts, I don't know why, or how, but it is absolutely clear to me that I have to forgive, if I want to survive.

Help me not to bottle up my pain or hide from it, but instead be like Dr Izzeldin Abuelaish and accept that what happened to me was God's plan. Cause the consequences of my life to lead to good, not to ever-increasing despair.

As I choose to forgive, free me! Make it clear that as I forgive, You immediately untether me from the yoke that bound me to the person who caused the harm. Free me so that I can grow and move forward in life, no longer a victim or a captive. As I forgive, unshackle my future from my past.

Amen.

Chapter Sixteen:
Some Final Thoughts

'God will make clear.'[1]
Paul, in letter to the Philippian Church

It's a strange feeling for me to be penning final words for a book that has consumed so much of my life for the past year or so. Every jot of ink on this page and on every page preceding it has been squeezed out of my own issues, questions and pain. I wrote it not to give you a definitive answer to solving life's greatest mysteries. I wrote this book to help you see that there is a pathway to hope.

It has definitely been a life-defining time for me. I have seen clearly enough to begin to rebuild the relationship with my dad, and that's pretty amazing. But rather than allowing me to somehow *get it all together* first, so that I could parcel up my new insights with a neat little bow and present them to you as the complete, inspired word from heaven on the matter, true to His character, God (in my life, at least) has made sure that I only saw it bit by bit and chapter by chapter, as I walked along the same messy road each one of us seem to have to walk.

Now, as we stand on the precipice of that future, I want to remind you that God has given us this life to live. So don't stop here but press on until you unearth more and more of God's treasure of a hope and a future.[2] The only way to ever know what the new way holds for any of us is to choose to hike it.

Having a desire for something new is great, but all the desire in the world will get you nowhere without an active turning from what was, to the *new way*. As so many will tell you, the old, well-worn way is safe. But it's only safe in the sense that you already know it and have experienced the pitfalls and gullies. Unfortunately, that safety net often stops all but the most adventurous of climbers. Novelist Lauren Oliver, put it this way, 'It's so strange how life works: You want something and you wait and wait and feel like it's taking forever to come. Then it happens and it's over, and all you want to do is curl back up in that moment before things changed.'[3]

I know that I will continue to have days where that desire to curl up back into the darkness will seem a million times easier than having to soldier onward and upward, through unknown feelings. And I know that it will be the same for you too. But on those days, we remember Paul's words to the Church of the Ephesians:

God has us where he wants us, with all the time in this world and the next to shower grace and kindness upon us in Christ Jesus. Saving is all his idea, and all his work. All we do is trust him enough to let him do it. It's God's gift from start to finish![4]

In one of his *Love Letters from Cell 92*, Dietrich Bonhoeffer wrote to Maria von Wedemeyer, 'How strange your life must seem to you these days. But one has to climb a mountain, too, in zigzags, or one would never reach the top, and from up there one can often see quite clearly why such a route was necessary.'[5]

Scripture is full of a hope-filled message – like this, which comes straight after the famous words of John 3:16, that 'God didn't go to all the trouble of sending his Son merely to point an accusing finger, telling the world how bad it was. He came to help'.[6]

And as Richard Rohr writes:

Once we can accept that God is in all situations, and can and will use even bad situations for good, then everything becomes an occasion for good and an occasion for God … There is nothing that God cannot and will not use to bring us to divine union – even sin … God's plan is so perfect that even sin, tragedy, and painful deaths are used to bring us to divine union. God wisely makes the problem itself part of the solution.[7]

I opened this book with a shockingly sad story of the senseless shooting of ten little girls in a schoolhouse in a quiet Amish community in Lancaster County, Pennsylvania. And it seems fitting to end there too, with whispers from the hearts of those special mums and dads who, as they muddled their way through that unthinkable experience, made a public declaration to forgive the shooter and his family. That statement left the watching world astounded.

Jonas Beiler, the author of the book about those families, drawing from the way they chose to live, writes:

You can wear your old hurts like a badge of honour, dragging yourself and others into a vortex of bitterness and anger. Or you can take the high road, the wise road, and like the Amish, tear down those old strongholds, rake the soil free of the debris that reminds you of your pain, and plant new seeds of friendship and grace. It won't be easy. And it will take time.[8]

And that is where our short time together ends. And as we go our separate ways, I commend you to God, with the prayer I opened the book with: May God Himself not only inspire you to *dream with your eyes open*, but also enable you to act on that dream… a dream of living a new and better way – a way where forgiveness is real, where healing is total and where God alone charts the road you take.[9] Holy Father, guard each one of us as we pursue this way, secure in the hope and knowledge that someday, as the old hymn says, 'He'll make it plain, someday I'll understand.'[10]

With love,

Post Scriptum

You never really understand a person until you consider things from his point of view, until you climb into his skin and walk around in it.[1]
Atticus Finch, To Kill a Mockingbird

Post Scriptum translates to our English word postscript, and is the PS you read at the end of a letter. It literally means *after having written*, which is exactly what this short note is. It comes many months after finishing the book. Since I finished writing the manuscript that became *The Great Embrace*, I have had the opportunity to do some profound personal soul-searching of my own … soul-searching over issues that I had to confront during the making of the Focus on the Family documentary *Irreplaceable* and while writing this book. One of the most pivotal issues, and probably the most asked about, is my dad and my relationship with him.

Amazingly, God has mended my relationship with my dad, but it wasn't until I took the time to consider his journey through his eyes, *to walk in his skin*. And that only happened because I was willing to acknowledge that God had a plan with the journey I was on, and as I allowed Him to carve, prune and shape my life and my story. Incidentally, God has also done unbelievable work on my dad's relationship with each of my brothers and sisters and, more miraculously, his relationship with Prue, my mum and his wife of over fifty years. They have both been though some deep counselling themselves, together and separately. I asked him to share some thoughts. These are his words:

My life has been a bit like a roller coaster ride, continuously up and down. It seems like I very often have to learn the hard way, and I continue to learn the hard way. But through it all, God has never been unfaithful to me. I have been unfaithful to my God, but He has certainly never let me down. He's always been there for me. I've always had a deep love for God and for Jesus, since I first met Him, but there are times when I have let Him down, very badly.

I often say to Prue that in retrospect, there is nothing I would change about my life. Nothing, in spite of all the things that happened to us. I don't think I would change it because in each of the bad situations that we've been through, God has a way of turning them around and using them for His glory and for our benefit. When you look at the lives of some biblical characters, you see the same sort of thing where they have gone through adverse life experiences, but God has used those very experiences to change them and they've come out better people, and strengthened.

Jesus came to set the prisoner free, and I experienced the truth of that scripture in my life. I came to understand the immense love and grace of God for each one of us – that God so loved us that He gave His only Son for me, a worldly, dishonest lawyer. He came to set me free, to bring me out of the prison darkness, and to give me the promise of a new life. And not only me, but my wife Prue, and also each member of our family, my father, my mother, my sister, my brother. We have all come to know Jesus![2]

Since my father made that statement, he has gone even deeper into his healing journey. After a lot of soul-searching, counselling and prayer, at the age of seventy-five years old, I saw him look my mum in the eyes and truly apologise. He said that for the first time in his life he was able to see just how selfishly he had lived his life. That is the power of God through a willingness to search and seek His truth. That power is also what led me to write a letter to Warren Sisarich that I thought I'd share with you here.

Dear Dad,

I don't know if I've ever told you this, Dad. You have shaped me… not just because of all the *hard stuff* that you put us through, but also because of your strengths. You are an incredible man in so many ways.

Dad, you taught me to love in spite of flaws and faults. You taught me how to give without expecting back. You taught me the real value of honesty and you taught me the real value of hard work – Mum told me that I could be all that I wanted to be, but it was you who taught me how to get there.

Dad, you showed me Jesus, and you taught me how to connect with Him. I will never forget the day you prayed for me to have the gift of tongues when I was four. Remember that?

Dad, you taught me how to respect God… His power and His grace. I saw that in you and I caught it.

Dad, you never used to say the words much, but I know you love me. I knew you loved me when you held me after I fell into that empty pool, when I went head first through the glass door and when I knocked myself out on that street. Dad, I saw love every time you stood on the sidelines of my rugby games.

You may not know it, Dad, but you are the one man who can

bring a sense of calm to me when things seem to be spinning out of control. Though your words are few, they are filled with wisdom and understanding.

Dad, maybe we should talk more about this love stuff. And maybe we should have spent more time showing it more clearly to each other. Maybe, this letter could be the start of all that.

Dad, you're the only father I've got and I love you… Happy Father's Day!

Tim.

There is so much I don't understand about God, but as I push on in this journey, this pilgrimage, I continue to see more and more threads of God-spun gold – signposts that remind me that I truly am loved and that He continues to encourage me to walk on.

If you want to know more about my personal story, the story of my dad and where our relationship stands today, a really good place to start is by watching *Irreplaceable*.[3] And also please feel free to drop me a note via www.timsisarich.com.

End Notes

Chapter One: An introduction

1. T.E. Lawrence and edited by Brad Berner, *Seven Pillars of Wisdom*, Kindle Edition (Amazon Digital Services, Inc.), 2010, p. 2

2. Quoted and paraphrased from a radio interview I did with Jonas Beiler and from his book *Think No Evil*, with Shawn Smucker (Brentwood, TN: Howard Books, a division of Simon & Schuster, Inc.), 2009

3. Jeremiah 29:11, HCSB

4. Jeremiah 29:11, HCSB

5. Luke 22:42, HCSB

6. Luke 22:42–44, *The Message*

7. Alexander Shaia, Michelle Gaugy, *The Hidden Power of the Gospels: Four Questions, Four Paths, One Journey,* Kindle Edition (Bedford, NH: Sophia Institute), 2001, p. 232

8. Lawrence and Berner, *Seven Pillars of Wisdom*, Kindle Edition, 2010, p. 2

9. Psalm 1:6, *The Message*

10. Matthew 6:9–13, *The Message*

Chapter Two: Know where you've come from

1. Leon Uris, *Mila 18*, Kindle Edition (NY: Open Road Media), 2011, p. 58

2. Nelson Mandela, *Long Walk to Freedom*, Kindle Edition (New York: Little, Brown & Company.), 1st edition, 2008, p. 544

3. You can find out more about the Truth and Reconciliation Commission at the official Truth and Reconciliation Commission Website – http://www.justice.gov.za/trc/ (accessed 1.11.16)

4. Mandela, *Long Walk to Freedom*, p. 544

Chapter Three: Unattainable desires

1. Jean C.J. d'Elbée and M. Teichert, *I Believe in Love: A Personal Retreat Based on the Teaching of St Therese of Lisieux*, Kindle Edition (Bedford, NH: Sophia Institute) Kindle Edition, 2001, p. 26 (They quoted it from *Manuscrits Autobiographiques*, p. 244)

2. Romans 8:28, NIV 2011 UK

3. Malachi 4:6, HCSB

4. *Irreplaceable* is a documentary produced by Pine Creek Entertainment in association with Focus on the Family in 2014. It's the first in a series of feature-length documentaries that approaches the concept of the family from a number of different angles. The goal of each documentary is to recover, renew and reclaim the cultural conversation about the family. *Irreplaceable* was written

by Glenn Stanton and Leon Wirth, produced by Michael O. Sajbel, Laurie Leinonen and John Shepherd and was directed by Tim Sisarich. It is part of Focus on the Family's *The Family Project*, a 12-session, DVD-based small group experience that digs deeper into the themes explored in *Irreplaceable* – http://www.irreplaceablethemovie.com (accessed 1.11.16)

5. Taken from Part One (The Profession of Faith), Section One ('I believe' – 'We Believe'), Chapter One (Man's Capacity for God), Point I (The Desire For God) of the Catechism of the Catholic Church – http://www.vatican.va/archive/ccc_css/archive/catechism/p1s1c1.htm (accessed 1.11.16)

6. John Chryssavgis, Kallistos Ware, Benedicta Ward, *In the Heart of the Desert: The Spirituality of the Desert Fathers and Mothers (Treasures of the World's Religions)*, Kindle Edition (Bloomington, IN: World Wisdom), revised edition, 2008, p. 36

7. Christopher West, *Fill These Hearts: God, Sex, and the Universal Longing*, Kindle Edition (NY: Image, an imprint of Crown Publishing Group, a division of Random House Inc.), 2008, p. 61

8. Taken from Part One (The Profession of Faith), Section One ('I believe' – 'We Believe'), Chapter One (Man's Capacity for God), Point I (The Desire For God) of the Catechism of the Catholic Church – http://www.vatican.va/archive/ccc_css/archive/catechism/p1s1c1.htm (accessed 1.11.16)

Chapter Four: What I cannot do

1. d'Elbée and Teichert, *I Believe in Love*, p. 28

2. Chryssavgis, Ware, Ward, *In the Heart of the Desert*, revised edition, 2008, p. 31

3. Jeremiah 29:11, NIV UK 2011

4. Uris, *Mila 18*, p. 492

5. R.T. Kendall, *Total Forgiveness: When Everything in You Wants to Hold a Grudge, Point a Finger, and Remember the Pain – God Wants You to Lay it All Aside*, Kindle Edition (Lake Mary, FL: Charisma House), revised edition, 2010, p. 1

6. Kendall, *Total Forgiveness*, p. 20

7. Luke 23:34, NIV 2011 UK

8. Matthew 27:51 tells us that at the moment when Jesus died on the cross, the temple veil was torn from top to bottom, allowing all to see the Holy of Holies, the fullest glory of God. I believe that this was a visual symbol of what the sacrifice of Jesus dying on the cross gave us - it allowed us into the heart and throne-room of God Himself; it allowed us to see God

9. St Augustine, F.J. Sheed, *Confessions*, Kindle Edition (Indianapolis, IN: Hackett Publishing Co.), 2nd edition, 2011, p. 83

10. Incidentally, God answering this mother's prayer meant that Augustine went on to become a saint to both the Catholics and Anglicans. Also, he is considered by many Protestant theologians to be one of the theological fathers

of the Protestant Reformation due to his teachings on salvation and divine grace. God used him to have a profound impact on our Christian faith, no matter what our particular theological bent. You can read the story in more detail in *Confessions*, ibid.

11. Pope Francis, *The Joy of the Gospel (Evangelii Gaudium): Apostolic Exhortation*, Kindle Edition (USCCB), 2014, p. 61

12. C.S. Lewis, *Mere Christianity (C.S. Lewis Signature Classics)*, Kindle Edition (HarperCollins e-books), revised & enlarged edition, 2009, p. 115. *MERE CHRISTIANITY* by C.S. Lewis copyright © C.S. Lewis Pte. Ltd. 1942, 1943, 1944, 1952.

13. Lewis, *Mere Christianity*, p. 116

14. John 3:17, *The Message*

15. D'Elbée and Teichert, *I Believe in Love*, Kindle Edition, 2001, p. 28

16. Pope Francis, *The Joy of the Gospel*, p. 61

17. Mother Teresa of Calcutta and Dorothy S. Hunt, *Love: A Fruit Always in Season* (San Francisco, CA: Ignatius Press), 1987, p. 77

18. See John 3:17, *The Message*

Chapter Five: The why to live for

1. This quote by Friedrich Nietzsche was taken from *Man's Search for Meaning*. Viktor E. Frankl, *Man's Search for Meaning*, Kindle Edition (Boston, MA: Beacon Press); 1st edition, 2006, p. 103

2. John 3:17, *The Message*

3. 'Begone, unbelief'. Words: John Newton (1725–1807), Olney Hymns (London: W. Oliver, 1779), number 37

4. I am referring here to Malachi 4:6, HCSB

5. Matthew 13:45–46, *The Message*

6. http://news.bbc.co.uk/onthisday/hi/dates/stories/january/27/newsid_3498000/3498330.stm (accessed 1.11.16), BBC, On This Day

7. Daniil Alexandrovich Granin, *Leningrad Under Siege: First-hand Accounts of the Ordeal*, Kindle Edition (Barnsley, South Yorkshire: Pen & Sword), 2012 (quotes referenced here were taken from throughout the book)

8. Alexandrovich Granin, *Leningrad Under Siege* (quotes referenced here were taken from throughout the book)

9. Alexandrovich Granin, *Leningrad Under Siege*, p. 155

10. Steve Brown, *A Scandalous Freedom: The Radical Nature of the Gospel* (NY: Simon & Schuster), 2004, p. 216

11. Taken from Isaiah 61:1–3, HCSB

12. Ignatius of Loyola (translated by Louis J. Puhl), *The Spiritual Exercises of St Ignatius* (Chicago, IL: Loyola Press), 1968, p. 13

13. 'Breathe' from the album *The Brilliance* by The Brilliance. Released 2010 (used with the permission of The Brilliance)

14. Psalm 119:105, NIV 2011 UK

15. Immaculée Ilibagiza, *Left to Tell: Discovering God Amidst the Rwandan Holocaust*, Kindle Edition (London: Hay House), 2007, p. 114

16. Ilibagiza, *Left to Tell*, p. 114

17. "As he went along, he saw a man blind from birth. His disciples asked him, "Rabbi, who sinned, this man or his parents, that he was born blind?" "Neither this man nor his parents sinned," said Jesus, "but this happened so that the works of God might be displayed in him." John 9:1-3, NIV 2011 UK

18. *The Didache* or *The Teaching of the Twelve Apostles* (Didachē means 'Teaching') is believed to be the work of the Apostolic Fathers of the early church, written between A.D. 70 and A.D. 100. It was almost included in the New Testament by the Council of Nicea, as it was considered by many to be the earliest Christian Catechism. It was lost to the church until a Greek manuscript was rediscovered in 1873.

19. *The Didache: The Teaching of the Twelve Apostles* (Santa Rosa, CA: BooksAndSuch) 2009, p. 1

20. Based on 'Breathe' by The Brilliance. Released 2010, ibid.

21. 'Breathe' by The Brilliance. Released 2010, ibid.

Chapter Six: You'll enjoy heaven that much more

1. Ron Leshem (translated by Evan Fallenberg), *Beaufort*, Kindle Edition (NY: A Delacorte Press book, Bantam Dell, A Division of Random House Inc.), 2008, p. 133

2. Lesham, *Beaufort*, ibid.

3. Mark 14:36, *The Message*

4. Matthew 6:9–13, *The Message*

5. Luke 9:23–25, *The Message*

6. Luke 9:23, HCSB

7. Romans 8:27–30, *The Message*

8. John 9:2, NIV 2011 UK

9. Isaiah 53:3, NIV 2011 UK

10. John 9:3, KJV

11. John 9:3, *The Message*

12. Genesis 50:20, HCSB, italics mine

13. Isaiah 45:6-7, NIV 2011 UK, italics mine

14. Miroslav Volf, *Exclusion & Embrace: A Theological Exploration of Identity, Otherness, and Reconciliation*, Kindle Edition (Nashville, TN: Abingdon Press), 2010, p. 9

15. Paraphrased from Proverbs 16:9

16. Isaiah 45:7, NIV 2011 UK

17. Proverbs 16:9, *The Message*

18. I found this quote in a daily reading – http://www.sacredspace.ie/daily-prayer/2015-08-28, accessed 1.11.16. Their source was Brian Grogan, *Finding God in All Things* (Dublin: Messenger Publications; 2nd edition, 2014)

19. Job 42:7, HCSB
20. From Psalm 139, *The Message*

Chapter Seven: He came to help
1. John 3:17, *The Message*
2. http://www.irreplaceablethemovie.com (accessed 1.11.16), ibid.
3. Proverbs 29:18, *The Message*, italics mine.
4. Pope Benedict XVI, *Saved in Hope*, Kindle Edition (San Francisco, CA:Ignatius Press), 2008, p. 9
5. Philip Yancey, *Where Is God When It Hurts?*, Kindle Edition (Grand Rapids, MI: Zondervan), Anv edition, 2010, p. 31, p. 33
6. Madeline Sheehan, *Unbeautifully* (Undeniable) (Volume 2) (CreateSpace Independent Publishing Platform), 1st edition, 2013, p. 1
7. C.S. Lewis, *The Problem of Pain*, Kindle Edition, (HarperCollins e-books). 1st edition, 2009, p. 90. *THE PROBLEM OF PAIN* by C.S. Lewis copyright © C.S. Lewis Pte. Ltd. 1940.
8. Leshem (translated Fallenberg), *Beaufort*, Kindle Edition, 2008, p. 348
9. James 1:2–4, HCSB
10. James 1:2–4, *The Message*
11. Pope Benedict XVI, *Saved in Hope*, p. 7
12. Romans 8:22-25, *The Message*
13. Psalm 23:4, KJV
14. Arthur Kleinman, *What Really Matters: Living a Moral Life amidst Uncertainty and Danger*, Kindle Edition (Oxford: Oxford University Press), 1st edition, 2006, p. 45
15. John 3:17, *The Message*
16. C. Baxter Kruger, *Jesus and the Undoing of Adam*, Kindle Edition (Jackson, MS: Perichoresis Press), 2001. Kindle location 89 of 1004
17. Kruger, *Jesus and the Undoing of Adam*. Kindle location 101 of 1004
18. Hebrews 12:1–3, *The Message*
19. Psalm 139:23–24, *The Message*
20. John 3:16, *The Message*
21. John 8:12, *The Message*
22. Taken from Psalm 30, *The Message*

Chapter Eight: Profit of suffering
1. This is from a poem written by Cardinal John Henry Newman and was taken from *The Father Gilbert Prayer Book* by Father Gilbert Hay (Silver Spring, MD: Trinity Missions), 1965
2. According to the Churchill Centre's website – (http://www.winstonchurchill. org/learn/speeches/quotations/quotes-faq (accessed 1.11.16), the speech was made on 29 October 1941 to the boys of Harrow School. The full speech is contained in *The Unrelenting Struggle* (London: Cassell and Boston, MA: Little,

Brown & Co. 1942, and is found on pages 274–76 of the English edition). It may also be found in *The Complete Speeches of Winston S. Churchill, edited by Robert Rhodes James* (New York: Chelsea House Publishers), 1974

3. Taken from Hebrews 12, *The Message*

4. Job 42:1–6, *The Message*

5. Hugh Ross, *Hidden Treasures in the Book of Job: How the Oldest Book in the Bible Answers Today's Scientific Questions* (Reasons to Believe) (e-book edition) (Grand Rapids, MI: Baker Books, a division of Baker Publishing Group), 2010. Taken from the book's Prologue

6. 'She'll be right, mate' is an Australian and New Zealand expresses that means that whatever is wrong will sort itself out, with a little bit of time.

7. Paraphrased from Revelation 21:4

8. John 14:6 (KJV; *The Message*; HCSB)

9. From John 15, *The Message*

10. Isaiah 53:3

11. Psalm 27:14, *The Message*

12. Quoted from Romans 7:24 – 8:39, *The Message*

13. Hebrews 11:39 –40, *The Message*

14. Hebrews 12:5–7,28–29, *The Message*

15. Hay, *The Father Gilbert Prayer Book*, ibid.

Chapter Nine: My idea of God

1. C.S. Lewis, *A Grief Observed*, Kindle Edition (HarperCollins e-books), 1st edition, 2009, p. 51. *A GRIEF OBSERVED* by C.S. Lewis copyright © C.S. Lewis Pte. Ltd. 1961. Published by Faber and Faber Ltd.

2. Luke 22:42, HCSB

3. Paulo Coelho, *The Alchemist – 10th Anniversary edition*, Kindle Edition], (HarperCollins e-books), 1st edition, 2009, p. 78

4. Job 12:10, HCSB

5. Isaiah 41:13, *The Message*

6. Deuteronomy 31:8, *The Message*

7.William Wilberforce, *Real Christianity*, revised and edited by Bob Beltz (Grand Rapids, MI: Regal Books), 2006, pp. 19–20

8. Job 1:1, *The Message*

9. From Job 40, *The Message*

10. Isaiah 45:9–10, HCSB

11. Ephesians 2:7–10, *The Message*

12. Jeremiah 29:13, *The Message*

13. Deuteronomy 4:29, *The Message*

14. Deuteronomy 4:29–31, *The Message*

15. Luke 11:9–10, *The Message*

16. Jeremiah 29:13, *The Message*

17. Isaiah 48:10, *The Message*

18. Quote taken from a sermon by the Rev. C.H. Spurgeon (No. 35), delivered on Sabbath Morning, August 12, 1855, at New Park Street Chapel, Southwark – www.romans45.org/spurgeon/sermons/0035.htm (accessed 1.11.16)
19. Lewis, *A Grief Observed*, taken from the book's introduction
20. Ibid., p. 51

Chapter Ten: Make a new ending

1. Michelle Cohen Corasanti, *The Almond Tree*, Kindle Edition (Reading: Garnet Publishing), 1st edition, 2012, p. 115
2. Joseph was the favoured son of Jacob, which angered his brothers. Genesis 37 tells us that they threw him into a well and then sold him as a slave. They told Jacob that Joseph was killed by beasts. However he ended up in an Egyptian prison where, eventually, the pharaoh found him and asked him to interpret his dream, That interpretation gave Joseph his freedom and a huge amount of power and control in Egypt. That position enabled him to save his family and the people of Israel from a terrible famine.
3. Blaise Pascal, *Pascal's Pensées*, Kindle Edition (Boston, MA: E.P. Dutton & Co., Inc.), 1958, p. 4
4. 1 Corinthians 2:9, NLT
5. Just before Jesus breathed his last breath on the cross, in John 19:30, he cried out tetelestai, which literally means, 'it is finished.' But the context in which the word was used during the time of Christ is fascinating - tetelestai was written on receipts when the debt had be paid in full or written on a convict's ledger when they had fully served their time. It meant that the price was fully paid and no one could accuse them of that debt or crime ever again.
6. Mark 12: 28-31, HCSB

Chapter Eleven: Forgiveness is power

1. Jacques Philippe, *Interior Freedom*, Kindle Edition (Strongsville, OH: Scepter Publishers), 2010, p. 63
2. Ibid, http://www.irreplaceablethemovie.com, accessed 1.11.16
3. 'The Return of the Prodigal Son' was painted by Rembrandt Harmenszoon van Rijn c. 1669. It's eight and a half feet tall x six and three-quarters' feet wide
4. 2 Samuel 22:25, *The Message*
5. Job 1:21, NIV
6. This quote from Nobel Prize winner Aleksandr Solzhenitsyn was taken from Gary Morsch, *The Power of Serving Others: You Can Start Here Where You Are* (Surry Hills, NSW: Accessible Publishing Systems PTY, Ltd.), 2008, p. 128
Solzhenitsyn originally wrote the words in *The Gulag Archipelago* 1918–1956. Aleksandr Solzhenitsyn wrote *The Gulag Archipelago* between 1958 and 1968. It is based on Solzhenitsyn's own experiences as a gulag prisoner as well as from eyewitness testimony from other prisoners. It was first published in the West when the Soviet Union was firmly behind the Iron Curtain. Underground

publications of the book did made its way into the USSR before the breakdown of communism.

7. Lewis, *The Problem of Pain*, Preface page

8. 'A catechism is the name given to a written work that contains a summary of all the beliefs of the faith that is used as a teaching tool. Until the second half of the twentieth century, for millions of Catholics in the United States the word catechism meant the Baltimore Catechism, which originated at the Third Plenary Council of Baltimore in 1884 when the bishops of the United States decided to publish a national catechism. The Baltimore Catechism contained 421 questions and answers in thirty-seven chapters and gave unity to the teaching and understanding of the faith for millions of American Catholics. Its impact was felt right up to the dawn of the Second Vatican Council in 1962. Quoted from the United States Conference of Catholic Bishops' – http://www.usccb.org/beliefs-and-teachings/what-we-believe/catechism/ (accessed 1.11.16)

9. Quote was taken from the Centre for Action and Contemplation website and is quoted directly from Richard Rohr's Daily Meditations. It was originally adapted from the audio presentation, 'Eucharist as Touchstone', Richard Rohr's teaching/reflection at the 2000 New Mexico Eucharist Congress – http://myemail.constantcontact.com/Richard-Rohr-s-Daily-Meditations--Make-Sure-You-Are-Hungry----Transformation----August-8--2013. html?soid=1103098668616&aid=RKQqaj_20TE (accessed 1.11.16)

10. Joshua 1:9, KJV

11. Psalm 97:11, *The Message*

12. Romans 8:35–39, *The Message*

13. Philippe, *Interior Freedom*, p. 63

14. Hay, *The Father Gilbert Prayer Book*, ibid.

Chapter Twelve: The bravest thing

1. Brené Brown, *The Gifts of Imperfection: Let Go of Who You Think You're Supposed to Be and Embrace Who You Are*, Kindle Edition (Center City, MN: Hazelden), 2010, Preface

2. Proverbs 3:5–6, HCSB

3. From Proverbs 3:5–6, *The Message*

4. 2 Corinthians 5:17, *The Message*

5. Matthew 22:37, *The Message*

6. Ephesians 1:1, *The Message*

7. Ephesians 1, *The Message*

8. Archbishop Desmond Tutu and the Reverend Mpho Tutu, *The Book of Forgiving: The Fourfold Path for Healing Ourselves and Our World*, Kindle Edition (NY: HarperOne), 2014, p. 38

9. From Psalm 19:7-9, *The Message*

10. Based on Ephesians 1, *The Message*

Chapter Thirteen: God loves us as we are
1. Psalm 139:14, *The Message*
2. R.T. Kendall, *Totally Forgiving God: When it Seems He Has Betrayed You*, Kindle Edition (Lake Mary, FL: Charisma House), 2012, p. 189
3. Matthew 22:37, HCSB
4. Matthew 22:37, *The Message*
5. Ruth-Alice von Bismarck and Ulrich Kabitz (translated by John Brownjohn), *Love Letters from Cell 92, The Correspondence Between Dietrich Bonhoeffer and Maria von Wedemeyer, 1943-1945* (Nashville, TN: Abingdon Press), 1995, Foreword
6. Von Bismarch and Kabitz, *Love Letters from Cell 92*
7. Ibid (italics added).
8. Ibid.
9. 1 Corinthians 1:26–31, *The Message*

Chapter Fourteen: Start Here
1. Brown, *The Gifts of Imperfection*, p. 48
2. Matthew 22:37–40, *The Message*
3. Matthew 25:21, NIV
4. James Martin, *Becoming Who You Are: Insights on the True Self from Thomas Merton and Other Saints*, Kindle Edition (Mahwah, NJ: Paulist Press), Christian Classics edition, 2013, p. 58, p. 23
5. Walter Kasper, *Jesus the Christ* (New York: Paulist Press), 1977, p. 86
6. Brennan Manning, *All Is Grace: A Ragamuffin Memoir*, Kindle Edition (Colorado Springs, CO: David C. Cook), new edition, 2011, p. 193
7. Brennan Manning, *The Wisdom of Tenderness: What happens when God's fierce mercy transforms our lives*, Kindle Edition (HarperCollins e-books), reprint edition, 2010, pp. 157–158
8. Brennan Manning, *A Glimpse of Jesus*, Kindle Edition (HarperCollins e-books), reprint edition, 2010, p. 22
9. John 8:36, HCSB
10. From 1 Corinthians 15:55–57, *The Message*

Chapter Fifteen: Be free!
1. Tutu and Tutu, *The Book of Forgiving*, p. 58
2. Job 1:20–21, HCSB
3. Job 1:22, HCSB
4. 1 Corinthians 13, NIV
5. John 16:33, *The Message*
6. Gregory David Roberts, *Shantaram*, Kindle Edition (NY: St Martin's Press), reprint edition, 2004, p. 468
7. Izzeldin Abuelaish, *I Shall Not Hate: A Gaza Doctor's Journey on the Road to Peace and Human Dignity*, Kindle Edition (London: Walker Books), 1st

edition, 2011, pp. 175–177
8. Abuelaish, *I Shall Not Hate*, p. 198, p. 212
9. Ibid., p. 196
10. Luke 6:35–38, *The Message*
11. Tutu and Tutu, *The Book of Forgiving*, p. 21
12. Malachi 4:6, HCSB

Chapter Sixteen: Some final thoughts
1. Philippians 3:15, NIV
2. Jeremiah 29:11, NIV
3. Lauren Oliver, *Delirium (Delirium Series Book 1)* (NY: HarperCollins), reprint edition, 2011, p. 44
4. Ephesians 2:7–8, *The Message*
5. von Bismarck and Kabitz, *Love Letters from Cell 92*
6. John 3:17, *The Message*
7. Richard Rohr, *Eager to Love: The Alternative Way of Francis of Assisi*, Kindle Edition (Cincinnati, OH: Franciscan Media), 2014, p. 10, p. 14, p. 11
8. Beiler with Smucker, *Think No Evil*, p. 208
9. Psalm 1:6, *The Message*
10. Lydia S. Leech, Adam Geibel, 'Someday He'll Make It Plain'

Post Scriptum
1. Harper Lee, *To Kill a Mockingbird* (Harperperennial Modern Classics), Kindle Edition (London: Harper), 2014, p. 39
2. My father's story appears in the book *Passing Through Shadows* by Ken Gartner, self-published by Ken Gartner, 2012. Used with permission
3. Ibid, http://www.irreplaceablethemovie.com (accessed 1.11.16)